GW00854865

THE NEW WINDMILL SERIES

General Editors: Anne and Ian Serraillier

182

A Wedding Man is Nicer than Cats, Miss

A Wedding
Man is Nicer
than Cats, Miss

rachel scott

heinemann educational books

Heinemann Educational Books Ltd
22 Bedford Square, London WC1B 3HH

LONDON   EDINBURGH   MELBOURNE   AUCKLAND
HONG KONG   SINGAPORE   KUALA LUMPUR   NEW DELHI
IBADAN   NAIROBI   JOHANNESBURG   KINGSTON
EXETER (NH)   PORT OF SPAIN

ISBN 0 435 12182 0

© Rachel Scott 1971
First published by
David & Charles (Publishers) Ltd 1971
First published in the New Windmill Series 1974
Reprinted 1978, 1983

Printed and bound in Great Britain by
William Clowes (Beccles) Limited, Beccles and London

to colin

acknowledgements

Some of the material used in this book has been broadcast in BBC Woman's Hour and in programmes on Radio Four, and has appeared in *Contact,* the magazine of the Pre-School Playgroups Association. Permission to reprint it is most gratefully acknowledged.

Contents

Foreword

by Sybil Marshall
author of EXPERIMENT IN EDUCATION and ADVENTURE IN CREATIVE
EDUCATION

'How far that little candle throws its beams!'

There's a cynical old proverb that when poverty comes in at the door, love flies up the chimney. We might be forgiven today for rephrasing it into something like 'When prejudice enters the lift, tolerance jumps off the roof'. The advent of a significant number of coloured immigrants, and their accumulation in large cities as opposed to even distribution throughout the country, has presented a new situation to which we have previously not been accustomed. As the numbers grew, we were aware of questions that needed answering, of differences and difficulties; these were human questions about day to day existence, and the difficulties of adjusting to each other's different cultures, when people of different races, colours and beliefs had to live in close proximity. Then politics—on both sides—stepped in, and commonsense departed. 'Questions' have become 'problems', to which 'solutions' are 'demanded'; arguments have turned into 'causes' and 'difficulties' spell 'trouble.' 'Differences' changed to division, and controversy such as 'freedom' and 'equality' have become dangerous in the mind and dynamite on the tongue, for they generate emotional energy that is released in impassioned oratory, virulent journalism, banner-waving 'demos' and private violence in the back streets.

Such intolerance—again on both sides—is largely due to fear, and fear in its turn is largely the result of ignorance. The ignorance in this context is perhaps of the very worst kind, for it exists not because the people concerned cannot know but because they choose not to find out. Meanwhile the innocent suffer, and this group consists mainly of children and young people. The little children, too young to know the meaning of tolerance and intolerance but quite old enough to suffer hurt and indignity, are helpless victims of circumstances into which they have found themselves born. While the intolerance bred of prejudice—on both sides— taints the very air they breathe, it is unlikely that they can, or will, grow into teenagers who can work or play together, or men and women who can become sensible citizens able to regulate and control their personal likes and dislikes for the benefit of their common humanity.

But ignorance, and children, are the province of education, and to education we turn for the tiny spark of light that, like Portia's candle, throws its beams very far into a dark world.

While 'causes' rage and violence threatens, there are ordinary people caught up in the day-to-day practicalities of living together, doing the jobs they chose as their careers in circumstances very different from what they envisaged, having to make rapid adjustments as the pattern changes from day to day, and having to learn, quickly and thoroughly, the lessons each day teaches them. These are the teachers in the schools in the towns where the coloured immigrant population is really large enough to be significant. While sociologists—of both sides—have a field day and produce statistics to be bandied about and twisted to serve whatever purpose hot-headed orators have in mind, the teachers, particularly in the inner city primary schools, are concerned with the day to day fate of the little figures, black, brown or white, sitting in front of them or playing around them.

The authors of this book and 'Infants Miss' are two such people, not 'two ordinary teachers simply doing their job,' for they are anything but ordinary by any standard. Nevertheless they would make no large claims that they were doing things very different from many others. What they did that was perhaps 'different' was to be aware all the time of what

12

they were doing, why they were doing it, how they could improve it, what they were succeeding in doing for the children in their care, and last but by no means least, what the children in their turn were doing for them. What is more, they took the trouble to record it, and the result is here before us in one of the most illuminating and heart-warming educational documents I have ever come across.

On every page their difficulties are recorded, with their solutions to the multitude of tiny practical problems—such as the confusion caused by a different system of name-giving —that together accumulate into the 'differences' that in turn cause the prejudice and intolerance. The book tells, with humour and detachment, the children's views of themselves and of the culture they (we) had previously felt to be so unassailable. As one follows the story, one becomes aware of the progress of true understanding among the cultures, *and of attempts on both sides* to further this. The efforts of these dedicated teachers to understand their charges brought them in touch with the adult communities to which the children belonged. Mothers and fathers came willingly, even eagerly, to learn from their children's teachers. The teachers, equally willingly and even eagerly, accepted personal invitations to homes and ceremonies that deepened still further their understanding of the adjustments still to be made.

'A little leaveneth the whole.' Perhaps the most heartening chapter of all is the one that tells the story of the day's outing to the sea, and of the children's gradual conquest of the all-too-ready-to-be-prejudiced coach driver. He was, one feels, an all too typical example of the person intolerant by reason of ignorance. Knowledge at first hand changed his opinion, at least of one batch of little immigrant innocents, and the upgraded opinion of 'the other side' was of course mutual. The children thought him a king among men. By his willingness to be persuaded out of his intolerance that day he may have saved much unhappiness and averted even misery and violence in the future.

13

From beginning to end of this book one is in the company of two extraordinary people. Everything described is, to me, educationally sound and could be used to great advantage in other schools in places where 'immigration' is still only a word heard on television and radio; but it is the warm-hearted, practical, commonsense-based approach to the urgent question of race relations that makes this book of such real importance to everybody, because every single one of us has a part to play in finding a peaceful answer to this question if anything any of us cares for is to survive. On any ground, it is a book with which I am honoured to have been associated.

June 1971   *Heathfield*
                                                        Sussex

Children with problems

I took a deep breath and opened the door. There were children everywhere, little ones and big ones, brown and oatmeal, coffee and cream, with plaits and without, some with topknots, others in turbans, and one half-buried under a trilby. The room seemed full of eyes, black-ringed and luminous. Boys with western haircuts pomaded flatly into place or standing on end like chimney sweeps' brushes, crowded together near the window. Girls with heads veiled and satin trousers beneath flowered or silver-embroidered tunics leaned decoratively on desks or squatted on the floor. Tiny boys dressed exactly like adults in little suits with little ties and little shirts gazed about them in wonderment. The muslins and brocades, the green and blue of the turbans, the jingling bangles, the swinging gold earrings, made a moving kaleidoscope of colour.

The noise was indescribable, high-pitched singing,

shrill chatter, even shouting, and none of it in English, for these were no ordinary children. All were from India or Pakistan. All had been uprooted from their homes and thrust into a pale, northern world where everything was baffling.

In the thick of the mêlée stood the cheerful young girl who had volunteered to teach them English and who had persuaded me to join her on the staff.

'We've only eighteen at the moment,' she had told me before term began. 'You can take the ten juniors and I'll have the eight infants, together with the two or three who'll come in September.'

The two or three had turned out to be twenty, and they were not all five-year-olds by any means. As I helped to sort out the newcomers, picking up babies and putting them on chairs, trying to find desks big enough for the older boys who were taller than I was, I realised the immense range of their ages, from tiny Shabna just 3ft 3in from sandals to fringe, to the two gentlemen by the door who, hands in pockets, the collars of their camel-hair coats turned up, belts knotted nonchalantly around their plump middles, surveyed the scene with rolling eyes.

Poor Shabna! Small and solemn in her new satin tunic and pink hair ribbons, she tried to fold her plump little arms, having been warned no doubt that this would be expected of her. Meanwhile little Gurmail, jaunty in gold braid and a royal blue blazer, was climbing up his brother's back with a hammer in his hand trying in vain to pin a drawing to the mounting board. Som Singh, little more than a yard high, but dapper and smart in his miniature city suit, trotted up and

16

down giving out pencils, paper and orders. Obviously he was an old hand.

Whether at a signal from him or in a burst of spontaneous goodwill, the other old hands, all seventeen of them, suddenly began to sing, and for my gratification shrilled their way through two unidentifiable nursery rhymes. Their applause for themselves was hearty and prolonged and ended in a burst of delighted laughter.

As I winkled out the children who were to be in my class and lined them up at the door I wondered where and how I was going to begin. I little imagined that within two short years this special and experimental English Department would have outgrown the school itself, that I should be responsible for its curriculum and organisation, and that this was to be the most rewarding experience of my life.

In the beginning the town had only three Indians, an elderly, bearded Sikh and his two lanky sons, travelling packmen who dragged their battered suitcases from door to door hawking silk-fringed mats, Indian scarves and gaudy ties. Every evening, chattering, gesticulating, their long overcoats flapping, they vanished into the maze of streets behind the station. 'Look!' said the children as they went by. 'The Indians!' for that was thirty years ago, when turbans were a phenomenon in the town and glaringly conspicuous amongst the flat cloth caps.

No one would comment on them now. No one would even turn to stare, for brown faces, turbaned heads and Punjabi chatter are as integral a part of the West Riding industrial scene as the mills and chimneys which created it. The social revolution which brought Asian

17

workers, first as isolated individuals, then in small groups and later in their thousands, crept upon the town so gradually that even those who were to be most affected by the change hardly realised that it was happening.

Most of the early arrivals were Indian Sikhs, who after a time were followed, and in greater numbers, by Pakistani Muslims. All came from the former province of the Punjab, which by the partition of 1947 was divided between India and Pakistan. All were prospectors, seeking more lucrative jobs and a higher standard of living than they could ever hope for at home, where a graduate might count himself lucky to have any work at all, where even a senior university lecturer could earn no more than £25 a month, and where a factory hand's weekly wage averaged only £2.50.

In the woollen mills, where weavers and spinners were becoming increasingly difficult to recruit, and in public transport, where there was a chronic shortage of drivers and conductors, the newcomers were a godsend. Their eagerness to work overtime, their cheerful willingness to take the night shift ('I couldn't run it at all if it wasn't for my Pakis,' one millowner told me) enabled firms to complete orders for the home market more quickly and to increase their exports, and in transport ensured the continuance of bus services which would otherwise have been curtailed.

Once established in jobs, groups of relatives and friends joined together to buy houses in that quarter of the town where property was most readily available, a decaying Victorian suburb from which the tide of gentility had ebbed away, and where the solidly built terraces, once prim and attractive in their symmetry, now stood neglected and forlorn. In the midst of them, black with the accumulated grime of seventy years, stood the school.

When in 1958 the first Indian children were brought for admission, solemn and shy, walking sedately behind their father, there was nothing in the modest event to indicate that a new and adventurous chapter in its history had begun. They spoke only Punjabi, but there seemed no reason why they should not pick up English naturally, and so they were placed in the class appropriate to their age.

Whilst numbers were small, no more than one or two in a class, all went well. Gradually they learnt the language by a natural process of absorption, and their presence placed no undue strain on the teacher, but as more and more arrived, a formidable problem began to build up. However willing they might be to help the newcomers, teachers already coping with large, unstreamed classes had neither time nor energy to spare for coaching an extra ten or twelve children who understood nothing that was said to them. In such a situation the Asian boys and girls lost the urgent incentive to learn English, played and worked together almost in isolation from the rest of the class, and chattered contentedly to each other in Punjabi.

Something would have to be done. The first idea was to withdraw all Indians and Pakistanis from their classes for part of each day, and to teach them English, a scheme tried out with varying success by most education authorities with a similar problem. In our own case, and in spite of goodwill and hard work, it was not satisfactory. When the head of the Infant Department suggested that all our Asians should be given an intensive English course in a special class, where they would stay until they could take their place in the main school, the headmaster, young and enthusiastic, agreed to give the plan a trial, and coaxed the Authority into providing a teacher.

The plan had much to recommend it. The newcomers would progress more quickly; they would have a goal, integration, at which to aim; and most important of all, their presence in an ordinary class would no longer hold back the English children, an aspect of immigration about which many parents were understandably worried. So the Special English Department was born.

Within a year this school within a school had expanded beyond recognition, and there were seven large classes. When a child's English was good enough he was moved into the main school with boys and girls a year younger than himself. If he lived in a different part of the town, for newcomers were beginning to settle outside our immediate neighbourhood, he came first to us, and when he was ready he was moved to the school nearest his home.

The problems these children had to face were psychological and social as well as linguistic. To be wrenched away from all that was familiar, and set down in a matter of hours in a land where not even words had meaning, was a traumatic experience even for older boys and girls. To a small child the shock could be catastrophic, as marked and as severe as that which might follow an accident. From a world of sunshine, heat and colour he was transported without preparation to the cold and damp of a northern winter.

From a close-knit village community he came to an industrial town where even his own father, separated from the family by two or three years of exile, was a total stranger. The small, perhaps primitive village house in which he had lived was replaced by a cavernous terrace house in a dreary street.

The effects of the change could be serious indeed, inertia, apathy, almost complete withdrawal. When we took a child's hand there was no answering pressure, when we spoke quietly, soothingly, there was no flicker of acknowledgement in the eyes. Even the most attractive toy aroused no response, the fingers made no attempt to grasp it and the arm fell down heavy as lead. The child stared blankly into space, refused to eat and might not speak for days even in his own language. The symptoms, in fact, resembled those of autism.

With some, and thirteen-year-old Iqbal was one of them, adjustment was a long slow process. In class he sat slumped in his chair staring straight before him, making no response of any kind, impervious to even the gentlest of approaches. Sometimes he would walk over to the window, stare out unseeingly at the hills, then touch the pane with the tips of his fingers. He moved like a sleep-walker, and in the playground stood motionless, hands thrust deep into his pockets, completely unaware of the whirling, shouting children all around him. For months he never spoke at all, and the psychiatrist feared that even if he recovered, his personality would be seriously impaired.

Healing came from an unexpected quarter. He fell in love with the library. It was quiet there and the long shafts of sunlight falling through the high windows seemed to act as a balm for his bruised mind. He began to walk about and touch the books, then to take them from the shelves and look at the pictures. I let him spend the day there, and one morning he went over to the wall and touched it.

'It's a wall,' I said encouragingly.

'It's a wall,' he repeated gruffly, and smiled for the very first time.

It was the breakthrough. I made him a work-book, with words and phrases and pictures all based on his beloved library and soon he was trying hard to speak English.

Library Miss, as he called her, made him honorary assistant and he must have been the only librarian in the business who could neither read nor write. He developed a passion for books and, hating to see them ill-treated, set up a repair service of his own. Pages upside down, backs to fronts, he glued and taped and trussed and splinted until the stock looked like diagrams in a First Aid Manual. He kept the shelves scrupulously tidy and in the interests of neatness rearranged all two thousand volumes in order of size, regardless of subject. 'Little ones begin here, big ones finish here,' he said proudly to Library Miss, who patted him warmly on the shoulder then fled to the staff-room to be revived with tea. On the day he left us for his secondary modern school he thrust two silk scarves into my hand, one for Library Miss and one for me, and wept as he said goodbye.

Two Pathans arrived one day from a primitive village on the North West Frontier speaking only Pushtu, a language which not even our children could understand. They were hysterical and frenzied with shock. No one could soothe or reassure them, no one could explain the peculiar things that were happening all around, no one could interpret their sobbing pleas for help. Their isolation was terrifying to see. For five interminable hours they cried, screamed, kicked, wrenched themselves again and again from our restraining hands and dashed into the playground, where they ran round in circles like frightened animals. Once they escaped into the busy street, darting between the traffic and running like wild things, their eyes and nostrils dilated with panic. The two young men who pursued and caught them returned with bitten, bleeding hands. The children, whom fear had made incontinent, were wet and dirty. But we forgot our aching shins and scratched arms in sheer pity when we saw the despair which overwhelmed them as they were carried back to the place of dread. Exhausted, defeated, and with tears of utter hopelessness pouring down their cheeks, they fell to the floor and prayed.

Equally pathetic were the two little girls thrust one morning into my room wearing pleated kilts reaching down to their ankles and skewered to their waists with safety pins. As soon as their escort left, they threw themselves on the floor and lay there, arms flailing, yelling and screaming at the pitch of their lungs. The class was thunderstruck. Motionless, pens poised, they stared at the pair as if they were demons from hell.

'Speak to them, Jagindro,' I implored. 'Tell them not to be frightened.'

Jagindro, standing well out of range of the kicking feet, addressed them in unconvincing twitters. The screams grew even louder.

'You try, Avtar,' I begged, and Avtar, advancing on them from the head end, let out such a roar that they were shocked into silence and let themselves be carried to the class they were to join.

Their story was a tragic one. Almost as soon as they arrived in England, their mother had been taken to hospital with incurable cancer. The children, one seven, one five, had been left by their loving but irresponsible father locked all day in the house with only apples for comfort. They were neglected, wild-eyed and dirty, their hair a tangled mass. They scratched themselves continually and with concentrated ferocity. 'Fleas and probably lice as well,' reported their teacher within minutes of their arrival in her class. 'Both!' said the school nurse who had been summoned to clean them up, and who patiently disinfected their heads whilst Miss knelt before them manipulating a hand-puppet in an effort to distract them and to stop their screams.

Such cases of extreme shock and neglect were fortunately rare. The period of recovery varied with individuals. Most of the children, even the smallest infants, faced their strange new life in silence and with dignity. A few were sodden with weeping or quiet with despair, but the majority showed amazing resilience and had settled within two or three days.

With the five-year-olds the period of shock was often followed by a noisy phase when the child behaved oddly, bidding for attention, breaking toys and equipment, cruising aimlessly round the room or deliberately disturbing groups at play, behaviour which could lead those unfamiliar with the problem to assume that he was backward. It was a time as disturbing for teachers as for children and it called for great patience and understanding.

Sometimes in the early years, children, generally

boys, brought over specifically to benefit from an English education, made the journey from India or Pakistan quite alone, mother having been left in the care of grandfather, and they were a cause of grave concern to teachers and welfare workers alike. In almost every case they came to join a wholly male household in which father, elder brothers, uncles, cousins and lodgers were on shift work, or left for the mill before seven in the morning, and except at weekends could give only minimal care to the homesick newcomers.

There were pathetic figures among them, emotionally if not physically neglected and deprived of mothering and affection, as their weary faces, their listlessness, their often chronic anxiety showed all too plainly. Forlorn little groups would arrive in the playground before eight o'clock and huddle in the shelter of a doorway, frayed coat collars turned up against the biting wind, the eldest with a key around his neck or clutched in a thin brown hand. Tiny brothers came stumbling behind them over the cobbles at a baby trot, shirts unwashed, coats and braces buttoned awry, hair uncombed. Going home at lunchtime to an empty house they had to make their own meal, and in the hands of these inexperienced cooks the process took so long that more often than not they were late for afternoon school. It was a worrying situation, but one which became less common as more wives arrived to join their husbands.

Unlike their mothers, the newcomers could not remain for weeks, even months, in the shelter of home. The journey to school was terrifying for children who had spent their lives in villages where transport was geared to the slow rhythm of the bullock cart or the bicycle. The walk from home, however short, led along paved streets lined with dark stone buildings which must all have looked alike. The traffic, swift, dense and noisy, was utterly bewildering, and they would either ignore it and plunge across the street with no thought of danger, or stand in frightened little groups on the pavement waiting for some kind passer-by to pilot them to the other side. Our warnings about being knocked down made no impression. Even if they understood, they took it for granted that if they were knocked down they would just get up again. The first in a family, or the first from a particular area, were the worst sufferers, since the second and subsequent children always had a brother, a sister or a friend to lead and guide.

We taught road safety continually and using every aid we could think of. We borrowed a real lollipop and demonstrated its use in the street outside, and frequently took our classes to practise crossing on zebras and at traffic lights. The police Road Safety Officer, who wherever he went saw Asian children ambling casually down the centre of the road, or zigzagging at random across main streets, shared our concern and came often with his walking doll, his talking Belisha beacon, which to their amazement spoke 'Indian', his bikes and trikes and miniature zebra crossings. He even attended evening classes in Urdu.

The Education Welfare Officer stood for hours by an arterial road taking a traffic census to strengthen our plea for a lollipop lady to be stationed at a murderously busy junction along the children's route. The authorities were at first unwilling to agree. They took the view that it was the parents' responsibility to see

26

families safely to school, not realising that an Asian mother had even less experience of traffic, and was even more afraid of it, than her youngest sons and daughters.

It was with relief that we handed over the task of instruction to the Asian colleagues who later joined us, for then we could be sure that the drills, if not always remembered, had at least been understood. Giving up much of their free time they recorded sound-tracks to accompany the films, and it was delightful to hear the earnest Sooty, the errant Sweep and Mary's little lamb repeating their kerb drill in impeccable Urdu and Punjabi.

If getting to school was a worry, getting there on time was an even greater strain, when mother herself might be indifferent to the clock or might not even have one in her kitchen. Even Asian adults of professional standing admit that they feel harassed by the western preoccupation with time and by our constant, and to them unnatural, insistence on punctuality. It may have been of no account in a Jullundur village, but the children had to learn that in England it mattered.

To the young ones in particular the divisions of the school day were incomprehensible. Playtime, milk time, dinnertime, home time . . . Not knowing which was which, and terrified of doing the wrong thing, they were in a state of constant and sometimes painful anxiety. In a child still unnerved and unsettled, this worry about time could become an obsession. Kaldip drove his teacher to distraction by following her everywhere, pulling at her sleeve and asking endlessly, 'Miss, what time is it? Is it playtime? Is it milk time?' He even invented times of his own to fret about. 'Is it tick time?' he would say, anxiously waving his sum book when she took out her red pencil.

Whenever they were dismissed we had to tell them clearly, and repeat to each individual, just why and where they were going. Thrust into coat and gloves and turned into the yard at ten-thirty, they assumed, naturally enough, that it was home time. Juniors, as well as infants, had sometimes had enough by playtime on their first morning and were glad of an excuse to nip off. 'Miss! Miss!' said a five-year-old urgently tugging at my skirt. 'One has escaped!'

Prefects had to be posted on sentry duty at the gates, but even then a few managed to elude us. It was extremely worrying to know that youngsters speaking no English, and certainly unable to find their way home alone, were at large in a busy town. Sometimes they were returned to us by the police, sometimes by the proprietors of Indian or Pakistani shops to which they homed like pigeons, and once the Education Welfare Officer found two five-year-olds in the queue at the Labour Exchange.

Dates and places, as well as times, were interpreted with an elasticity which was infuriating. Both parents and children showed the same vagueness, the same lack of concern, about medical appointments made for them by their doctors or by the school health service. If the card said nine o'clock, eleven o'clock or even six would do just as well. If 10 November was the appointed day, then the 8th or the 20th, or even 10 December, would be just as convenient.

Any and every appointment was a casual arrangement cheerfully entered into and just as cheerfully discarded. 'Their values are spiritual, not temporal,' said a forgiving colleague when a group of senior boys invited to her home had failed to turn up. It was strange to find that children who in school were reliable and intelligent had this same cavalier attitude to appointments, and that even the politest did not regard such lapses as a breach of good manners.

Though accustomed to extremes of climate, for the Punjab can be frosty and cold in winter, families were entirely unprepared for the fickleness of English weather. On days when the sky was overcast and clouds gathered on the hills, infants would arrive shivering, teeth chattering, with not even a vest beneath dress or tunic. In the heaviest of downpours, boys and girls who had macs and hoods at home would come without them and arrive with water dripping from their hair. Did they, we wondered, expect to dry out as quickly as they would have done in the sunshine of India? If so, it took more than one drenching to get the message across. We had to plead and insist and even lose our tempers before children with waterproof clothing could be persuaded to wear it.

Every time a father brought his family for admission I stressed the importance of warm and waterproof outer garments.

'Get one with a topee,' I would say, holding out a duffle coat. 'Or with a zip,' pointing to an anorak.

'Oh, yes, sir!' he would reply (most fathers called me sir). 'I will get one for this boy this week and that boy next week,' and he almost always did.

Snow sometimes falls in the Punjab, especially in the north where the foothills of the Himalayas reach down into the plains, but never with the weight and persistence so familiar in the Pennines. The first snowfall of the winter took the children completely by surprise and their delight was lovely to see.

'Look out of the window,' I would say. 'It's snowing,' and silent for once, their eyes wide with wonder, they would gaze at the whiteness outside. Once when I opened the window and let the whirling flakes blow into the room, they stood up and welcomed them with wide-flung arms. 'Snow on me!' they called. 'Oh, snow on me!'

There was none of the noisy excitement with which an English class greets the arrival of snow, but a quiet almost reverent appreciation. They walked home through the drifts in a daze, unaware that their feet would soon be sopping wet. None of us had thought to tell them that snow would melt, and my room was full of puddles from the half-melted snowmen brought in to show me. The first time little pools appeared under chairs we feared the worst, but investigation revealed that the drips were coming from pockets stuffed with snow collected to take home to mother.

Fog they had never seen before and they hated it. Even adults brought up under the glare of Indian skies sometimes confessed that their first encounter with a pea-souper had filled them with panic, half claustrophobia, half terror at the blotting out of familiar landmarks. No wonder the little ones were speechless with fear, and even older boys and girls went completely to pieces.

Once, fog cut short the Christmas party. It was something new in their experience and it filled them with a primitive dread. They came rushing back hysterical and with all sense of direction lost. We tried to calm them, and by grouping children from the same area together managed to get most of them on their way, escorting them in convoys as far as the main road and the familiar lights of the Indian shop.

On arrival in England both Sikh and Muslim girls continued to wear traditional Punjabi dress consisting of a long, straight tunic known as the kameez, and a pair of baggy trousers, the shalwar, which had a drawstring top and fitted neatly and tightly around the ankles. On the head, which must always be covered in public or in the presence of men, was a scarf of embroidered tulle or lace. The general effect could be delightful, since the trousers were made of gay, bright satin, the tunic of shining lamé or brocade, but these garments, so attractive in themselves, were quite unsuited to West Riding weather. The shalwar were often soaking wet and bedraggled, and many a lesson had to begin with a drying-out session, with a row of forlorn little girls parked on or around the pipes, all steaming gently round the ankles. The trousers, however wet, had to be dried *in situ,* for no teacher wise in immigrant work would readily separate the shalwar from its owner. To do so might bring an angry parent protesting that his daughter's honour had been outraged.

It was some time before parents realised that strong shoes and snowboots were a necessity, and in the winter months girls new to England would come paddling through slush and puddles in openwork plastic or vinyl sandals. The need to look attractive was responsible for much of this pretty but unsuitable footwear, and it was noticeable that boys were often more sensibly shod. Tahir would come marching proudly through the snow in sheepskin-lined boots whilst his sister

31

trotted behind in gold lamé slippers, the only kind she possessed.

In equipping their children to face a northern climate, mothers had one valuable asset. They were enthusiastic and accomplished knitters, and made beautiful multicoloured woollies, using two, three or even four colours in designs reminiscent of Fair Isle. No pattern, however intricate, seemed beyond their skill and all were knitted without printed instructions. They either invented a pattern or copied one they admired from the actual garment. Many of them did, in fact, buy English knitting leaflets in order to copy the pattern from the picture on the cover, since they could neither read nor follow the instructions.

Mothers and older sisters were equally adept with a sewing machine, making their own shalwar and kameez and most of their children's clothes. Some made English dresses for the little ones, but though neat and pretty they were often fastened at the back with safety pins or nothing at all, since many mothers were unfamiliar with press-studs, zips, or hooks and eyes; a lesson devoted to teaching senior girls how to insert and use them was time well spent.

In cold weather some mothers were over-cautious and sent their children to school so tightly cocooned in wool that they could sit and bend only with difficulty, but most parents soon came to terms with the climate and made sure that boys and girls were suitably and sensibly clad.

Punjabi dress, to which we had become so accustomed, aroused bitter controversy in the schools to which girls went when they left us. To head teachers who were sticklers for school uniform, and above all to the prestige seekers whose aim was to run their schools like grammar schools, the very sight of the shalwar was anathema. Having battled for years against jeans, they could not be expected to welcome an invasion of trousered legs in every colour of the rainbow. The more rigid among them attempted a direct prohibition, ignorant of the tenacity, the ferocity even, with which the devout Muslim adheres to a way of life which is inseparable from his religion. Girls were kept away from school, harsh words were spoken on both sides, and sometimes the Imam himself would intervene.

This question of the shalwar has become to schools what the turban is to some transport authorities. It has been debated at conferences and staff-meetings, discussed in liaison committees and aired in letters to the press. It is further complicated by the fact that Muslims themselves are not in complete agreement. The well-educated, those from the urban centres of Pakistan who, having lived for some years in England, are anxious to become westernised, and who may for that very reason be out of touch with the main body of their people, state categorically that the wearing of shalwar is a social custom of the Punjab area, not a religious obligation, and that it is not specifically ordained in the Koran. The Muslims from the villages remain unshaken in their belief that it is a binding religious duty, for the Koran clearly states that the female form must be hidden from male eyes to prevent immoral thoughts or actions. Some head teachers and some enlightened Education Authorities reached a sensible compromise and agreed that shalwar could be worn provided they were in the sober navy, grey or brown of the school uniform.

Where this concession was made it came as a relief to the girls who, caught between parental wrath on the one hand and academic inflexibility on the other, had been subject to considerable strain. Having never in their lives bared more than face, hands and feet in public, many of them shared their elders' outraged disgust at the immodesty, the blatant indecency of western fashions as represented by the mini-skirt, the bikini and the sleeveless summer dress. One of their mothers had even spat over the garden wall at an English neighbour innocently lying on the lawn in a sunsuit.

The dark-coloured shalwar also had the advantage of making these shy girls less noticeable in the street where unthinking boys, not really meaning to be unkind, would shout, 'Baggy breeches!' or 'Pyjama pants!' Though the taunts were not understood, they could make a sensitive child extremely unhappy.

The veil, worn by all Muslim girls when they first arrived, was a serious menace in the rough and tumble of a lively school. With one end floating free and the other wrapped round the neck it could so easily be caught in a swing door, or on a cloakroom hook or a piece of apparatus, with unpleasant consequences for the wearer. No accident of this kind actually happened, but there was always the fear that it might.

In the home, too, where both mother and children were unaccustomed to an open fire, unfamiliar with a gas-ring and totally unaware of the threat presented by the oil-heater, the veil was a potential hazard. The home, of course, was outside our jurisdiction, but in school we could exercise gentle pressure and persuade the girls to discard the veil altogether, or if this was

34

asking too much, to wear a headscarf instead, and finally to discard even that, at least indoors.

If integration is ever to become a reality, concessions will have to be made for some time to come. Our Authority was wise enough to realise that our particular Punjabi Muslims could not be divested of their shalwar overnight, and that teachers would have to be patient and tolerant in the hope that the next generation might be more western in outlook.

Decisions about dress and finery were difficult, sometimes delicate. Our job was not just to teach, but to enable the newcomers to fit happily and easily into a normal school, to work and play on equal terms with English children. It would have been cruel to send them out looking and behaving in ways that were conspicuous, for in the crude world of the playground those who are different, whether in colour, physique or dress, attract teasing and jeers. Customs which conflicted with accepted practice, or with the day to day running of a school, had therefore to be tempered, perhaps eliminated, for to many head teachers conformity, uniformity and routine are the very air they breathe.

Yet it was not desirable to manufacture a race of brown Englishmen, though that is the process envisaged by most of the people who talk so glibly about integration. Every racial minority has a right to its distinctive habits and culture, and exile creates a psychological climate in which these are nurtured even more carefully than in the homeland, synonymous as they are with national identity. We encouraged our children to retain all that was good of their own culture, and above all to be proud of being Indian or Pakistani, whilst encouraging them to conform to such western standards of behaviour as would enable them to take their place in the community without embarrassment to themselves.

The middle way was far from easy. Dissuasion, rather than prohibition, was the policy. When girls appeared with varnished nails, we reasoned as we should have done with an English class. Painted nails were not allowed in school but there was no reason why they should not be varnished at weekends.

Perfume was harder to deal with. Many of the staff found the cloying sweetness of their hair oil and their extremely pungent scents both sickly and distasteful, but to me at least that was not sufficient reason for imposing a ban. The boys, who would be most open to ridicule on this score, were told that though Englishmen could, and did, use scented toilet preparations, they drew the line at perfume, which was regarded as effeminate and would certainly prejudice their schoolfellows against them. However kind and tactful the explanation might be, it was distressing to have to make it, for this was, in fact, an interference with established Asian rights and customs. In general the children understood that our suggestions were put forward in their own best interests, but the role of censor was not an enviable one, especially when the boys came bearing gifts.

'This is a prisint for you,' said Arshad, holding out a tiny bottle of perfume made of cheap glass sealed at the top with cork and wax. It reminded me instantly of the miniature bottles of sweets on the shelves of my own toy sweetshop long ago. 'It is for your moustache,' he explained thrusting it into my hand. It was certainly meant to last, and even a fleeting contact with the stopper left my fingers tainted for days.

The use of eye make-up, so widespread in the East, came gradually to be discarded without any prompting from us. The overriding impression left by my first day at school had been that of myriads of black-ringed eyes. The custom was not merely an aid to beauty but a concession to superstition, as well as a precaution against infection. 'It keeps away evil spirits,' said Bindi when she brought me a tiny brass flask which held the fine black powder known as *surma*, used for centuries in the Orient to darken lids and lashes. Inside the screw top was a stopper which withdrew to disclose a small stick called a *surmchoo*, which fortunately was blunt at the business end. With this she proceeded to draw lines in my eyes, and *in* was the operative word, for unlike the eye-liner and brush technique of the western doe-eyed beauty, this powder was applied to the inner eyelid. It was a very painful process.

Even babies were eye-lined from the moment of birth. Friends in maternity homes reported that Asian mothers were frequently reprimanded by horrified sisters for painting the eyes of their offspring just as soon as the opportunity occurred. They regarded it as a sensible preventive measure against the eye diseases so prevalent in India.

Painted eyes could be attractive, but palms dyed with henna were disconcerting. The dye was generally put on after a celebration, perhaps a holy day, or after a betrothal, and the bright orange-red stain could not be removed by soap and water, nor even by vigorous scrubbing with detergents, as I found to my cost when, all unsuspecting, I allowed Jagindro to rub my palms

37

with a seemingly innocuous substance. 'It stays a very long time,' she said in tones of the utmost satisfaction. It did!

To critics of Asian ways these customs seemed pagan, even dirty, and were regarded as being on a different and inferior level of culture from their own dyed hair and painted lips, whilst as for nose-rings, they regarded them with horror, quite oblivious of their own pierced ears.

The girls attached great importance to the wearing of jewellery, and beads and bangles, rings and earrings flashed and jingled all around us. Even quite small girls had had their ears pierced, and not always by the most hygienic methods. A small, sharp stick had been used on at least one infant, but we hoped that this was the exception and not the rule. No one wore sleepers, but the ear-rings could be taken out and the holes plugged with tiny pieces of wood, which sometimes left an infection or a suppurating sore.

There was great reluctance to discard these feminine trinkets for it was a Pakistani girl's duty to look pretty, but some of the dangling ornaments would have to go, for to most headmistresses they were an abomination. To ban all jewellery all the time would have been impossible, and constant nagging would have vitiated the happy relationship between us. It seemed sensible to concentrate on those items which, like ear-rings, were a danger in school. On three occasions at least, ear-lobes were badly torn, even severed from the face, during Physical Education lessons, and there were rumours of similar cases elsewhere.

There was one particular ear-ring we left alone, a copper wire threaded through the pinna of the ear and twisted into a knot on the outside. It had been placed there, an Asian colleague explained, to cure 'any moving pain' the boy might have, perhaps the eastern version of the old belief, so recently revived in England, that the wearing of copper prevents the onset of rheumatism, or even cures it once it has been contracted. Although the wire was as dangerous as the girls' long ear-rings the doctor assured us that it was not doing any harm in itself. The parents were adamant that it should not be moved, so there it remained.

Bangles also were a risk, especially when their owners went swimming, for they were very fragile, and broken glass had caused many cut feet and scratched hands at the baths. So bangles, too, had to be vetoed.

Looking back on our numerous bans and prohibitions I realise now what a dismal, dowdy lot we must have seemed in our sober tweeds and cardigans, and what killjoys we had of necessity to be, for ever clamping down on all their pretty finery. No wonder they tried to brighten us up with frequent gifts of beads and of the controversial bracelets. I would look in dismay at my big square fist, so clumsy beside their fine-boned hands and tapering fingers. 'No! No!' I would cry as they tried to force the bangle over my knuckles and thumb joint, but with soap and determination, and by folding my thumb and fingers in a special way, they achieved their object. It was a knack I never mastered, and when at the end of the day I applied the process in reverse, the washbasin was always full of shattered fragments of rainbow glass.

The steel bangle, one of the symbols of Sikhism which every adherent of the faith is supposed to wear, was permitted not simply for religious reasons but because, having been put on the child at birth, it could not be removed. It was the *kara,* one of the 'Five Ks' which Gobind Singh, the last great guru, made his followers swear to observe. Spiritually it symbolises restraint, a 'moral handcuff,' and historically it may be derived from the ancient practice of fastening charms on the wrists of men about to engage in battle.

No attempt was made, either, to interfere with the minute silver replica of the Koran worn by many Muslims on a cord round the neck and sometimes protected by a little drawstring bag.

Customs such as these, definitely religious in origin and observance, were never challenged. No Sikh was ever asked to take off his turban, or pugree as it was called, or to cut his long hair, for the unshorn head, or *kesh,* was yet another of the 'Ks.' It is a custom for which Sikh historians have put forward a variety of reasons. Long hair was in the tradition of the great Indian mystics and ascetics, or perhaps the guru ordained it in honour of the goddess Durga, or to inspire fear in the enemy, or to be the symbol of virility and strength. He may also have meant it to set the Sikh apart from his Muslim and Hindu neighbours and to serve as a continual reminder of his faith.

Whatever the origin of the custom, it certainly set small Sikhs apart here in England. Little boys wore plaits tied with gay ribbons, and in the upper reaches at any rate were indistinguishable from little girls. Many were, in fact, mistaken for girls on admission, and confusion increased when little girls arrived with hair cropped like a boy's to stimulate its growth into long, thick plaits. Hosan, whose head was covered with short, black stubble, was entered as a boy and sent with an interpreter to the cloakroom. 'He's a girl!' reported the grinning Abdul a few moments later, and explained how a tumble of satin and an arm full of bangles had emerged from the enveloping duffle coat.

Orthodox Sikh families continued to obey Guru Gobind Singh's injunction as strictly in England as they would have done in the Punjab. When a small boy's hair had reached a certain length he was taken to the temple for the first ceremonial plaiting. Later the hair was wound into a topknot which looked very fetching, and which was so firmly secured by tape and pins that neither football nor fighting could dislodge it. It was often covered with a square of white cloth or a handkerchief secured with a rubber band, but we were always glad when this was voluntarily discarded, for it soon looked tatty and hung awry, making the boy conspicuous. 'Is that where you keep your marbles?' his English friends would ask, tapping it playfully with a knuckle.

He began to wear a turban when the hair became too long even for a topknot. The strip of material, five yards long and one yard wide, from which the pug was made, was wound skilfully round the head by a technique which had to be mastered. One pathetic little Sikh went about for months with his head looking like a bale of straw because his family had forgotten the knack, and had to await the return of an uncle from India to instruct them in the art.

What a commotion there was if ever a pug came undone in class! A dozen willing helpers sprang importantly to the rescue, all winding muslin around each other, all issuing contradictory instructions, whilst at the centre of the mad cocoon the owner, alternately blinded and throttled by the yards of enveloping material, shrieked louder than anyone.

The more sophisticated adult tied his pug and sprayed it with instant starch to keep it all in one piece, and to enable him to pop it on and off like a wig and he might also invest in a small polythene bag to protect it from wind and rain.

Many Sikhs did eventually cut their hair, often after the first swimming lesson, having discovered how uncomfortable it was to spend the rest of the day with wet, dangling locks, but the decision was always their own and was in no way influenced by us.

Small girls just beginning to grow their hair indulged in a little innocent deception by braiding thick, black Kashmiri wool into their still scanty tresses, creating a false plait which stretched down to their waists and ended in golden bobbles, or was interwoven with silver braid. These woolly plaits were almost indistinguishable from the real thing until they became detached in the fury of playtime or the scuffle of a netball game. 'Has anybody lost this plait?' the cry would go up from the monitors, parading what looked like a scalp-lock from room to room. But plaits could not always be reunited with their owners, and we must have had the strangest lost property room in the country.

In this world of school there was so much to remember, so much to be afraid of, and high on the list of hazards was the English lavatory. In the villages from which so many came, the only toilet facilities had been the bush, the tree and the hole in the ground, and even at school they had left their classes to relieve themselves in the fields. Here there were embarrassing

42

occasions, though happily rare, when junior boys and even girls were found performing without any sense of shame on a patch of grass near the caretaker's house. Only the few who had lived in towns had any knowledge of indoor sanitation. 'We had a proper toilet in our house,' said Mumtaz proudly. 'Every day somebody came to try it. My uncles, my aunties and my Daddy's friends. All the day it was flush! flush! flush! What a noise!'

Even the town dwellers, however, had been accustomed to squatting over a floor-level bowl and had never seen or used a pedestal toilet. Physical contact with a seat used by so many people seemed to them dirty and insanitary. The lavatory pan was a yawning abyss into which the little ones were terrified of falling, and the cataract when the chain was pulled sent them hurtling out, shalwar still at half-mast, as if devils were after them. Some experienced real difficulty in having a motion at all when seated, so accustomed were they to the more natural crouching position, and they found it safer to use the floor, a habit which sometimes created problems for the caretaker and his staff, or for the teacher on duty when they were not available. Some children stood on the seat and risked a nasty fall by doing so.

To orthodox Muslims, the western habit of wiping with toilet-paper appeared unhygienic compared with their own custom of washing imposed on them by the Koran. 'They allus take bottles o' watter to t' lav!' said an old lady with Muslim neighbours, and was surprised to learn that so odd a practice was ordained in their Holy Book.

It was imperative to retrain them so that they could

43

become socially acceptable both in school and in public places, for in factories and workshops where Asians are employed this misuse of the toilet is a frequent source of prejudice against them, and complaints that they soil the floor and break seats by standing on them are angry and widespread. The fact that habits which to us seem uncivilised may be social, or even religious, in origin, is rarely if ever explained.

I took every new child to the cloakroom with an interpreter, who gave a spirited demonstration in Punjabi; an artist friend produced a series of lively drawings to make our explanations doubly clear. Picture I showed a girl crouching on the floor beside a lavatory, but a thick black cross indicated that this was wrong. In Picture II another girl was standing on the seat, and a second black cross pointed out the error of her ways. Picture III bore a triumphant red tick, beneath which a paragon of virtue sat smugly in the correct position; there was, of course, a parallel series for the boys.

The habits of a lifetime are not easily broken and in spite of our endeavours, mistakes continued to occur. After one such accident I assembled the older boys and drew a lavatory on the blackboard.

'I'm very sorry, boys,' I began, 'but once again I have to talk to you about lavatories.'

'No! No!' chorused my young men politely. 'Don't be sorry!' and pointing to my sketch they said, 'It's a very lovelly laverterry!'

After playtime it was lovelier still, for an anonymous artist had added embellishments of his own, and swinging merrily from the chain was a turbaned Sikh.

Difficulties arising from religion were not at first

44

very apparent, but when children began to stay at school for dinner, customs affecting food became a source of worry, since even a modest meal was hedged about with religious taboos. Parents bringing boys and girls for admission would express deep concern about the observance of these rules, and their uneasiness was transmitted to their offspring who, for fear of offending, would often eat nothing at all, and whose perplexity was increased by the fact that everything on the plate before them was completely unrecognisable. Young children the world over are difficult about unaccustomed food, and the very sight and smell of a western meal could be revolting to a small Punjabi brought up on curry, rice and fruit. Some just wept as the peculiar dishes were set in front of them, and a few were actually sick, but most of them had a go, and soon conquered their aversion.

We were eager to help them, and at first it all seemed simple. Sikhs could not eat beef because the cow was sacred, and Muslims could not eat pork because in the Koran the pig was declared unclean, but the dinner ladies could not tell Sikh from Muslim. The worried brown faces filing past the hatch looked all the same to them, and the violent shaking of heads, the cries of 'No pig! No cow!' which marked their passage, made serving difficult. We gave them badges to wear, red for beef, green for pork, but the Muslims continued to be suspicious of luncheon meat, sausages, rissoles and pies, enigmas which might so easily be an offence against the faith, and they were even chary of eating mutton in case it had not been killed in the ritual manner. Notwithstanding our goodwill, difficulties multiplied. Some Sikhs were total vegetarians, and the

45

Hindus disclosed that they ate neither eggs nor fish, and there were always the imps who claimed exemption on religious grounds from any dish to which they had taken a dislike.

'Can't eat cabbage!' said one wide-eyed innocent on his first day at a new school. 'Muslims don't eat cabbage.'

If ever we felt confident that we, too, had mastered the rules, we would come across the occasional lapsed family who ate everything. For days our two Pathans fed exclusively on peas and salt. Salt, in fact, seemed popular with all religions and was smuggled out of the dining-hall in fistfuls until guards were appointed to check the traffic.

The meals organiser tried to ensure that the Asian children had balanced and nourishing meals, and got full value for money by substituting mutton for other meats and providing plenty of fish and extra vegetables. To her puzzled little clients, however, cauliflower and cabbage were strange messes, strangely cooked. Just as we ourselves were sometimes baffled by the unknown food served up to us by Asian friends, so the children shuddered when lids were lifted and for the first time in their lives they looked on, and smelt, steamed fish and boiled greens.

Meat was not their only aversion. 'Seconds' could be just as unpalatable. They disliked most of the traditional English desserts with the exception of puddings, which were provided for them in quantity. Chocolate and any dish tainted with it they loathed. Trifle filled them with disgust, a reaction which might well be ours if we were not so familiar with its mixed-up messiness. Fruit was welcome when it could be seen to be fruit,

46

but hacked up in fruit salad it was poked and sniffed and generally refused, whilst lurking under custard it was wholly unacceptable.

Knives and forks could add to the ordeal of eating, for Punjabi villagers manage admirably without such clumsy aids. Tearing off a piece of chupatti, the large, wholemeal pancake which is the unleavened bread of Asia, they roll it up and use it as a spoon, scooping up curried chicken, mutton or even goat. When it gets soggy they eat it and tear off another piece, thus consuming their cutlery as they go along. Most of the newcomers, eager to please, struggled valiantly to learn the new techniques, watching and imitating their English neighbours, and we tried always to remember that a child's reluctance to eat might well be due to its inability to handle a knife and fork. The very young would give up halfway in sheer discouragement.

New food, new manners, new implements, made the dinner-hour a trial for everyone. Their high-pitched voices, and the fuss they sometimes made in front of honest cod and irreproachable fruit jelly, generated a constant hubbub. I say generated rather than made, because the major babble actually came from the English who, under cover of this shrill Punjabi, made the most of their opportunities. A reprimand or an order given by the teacher on duty would be blandly ignored by the Asian contingent, *some* of whom had genuinely failed to understand. A ticking-off was often mistaken for a prayer. Seeing the dinner mistress grave and stern, interpreting her solemn warning as a call to devotion, the infants would bow their heads, screw up their eyes and put their hands together in the belief that grace was being said. They prayed earnestly through many a wigging and must have formed a strange idea both of us and of God.

The collection of dinner money was a nightmare. The simple request, 'Who is staying for dinner?' rarely brought a simple or accurate answer. I had to ask each child individually.

'Are *you* staying at school for dinner, for—er—for chupattis?'

'Have *you* brought any money?'

Some said yes if they thought I wanted a yes, but had no money. Some said no and produced the correct amount. Juniors and seniors brandished £5 notes for relatives in other classes, and added to the turmoil by demanding change of which we never had enough. Infants who had been paid for by older brothers and sisters denied that they were going to stay at all, and intimated to an interpreter that even force could not detain them on the premises. Many did, in fact, run away at the crucial moment, pursued by agitated monitors.

Before leaving each room I would subject the class to a final grilling, and make a last dramatic appeal. 'Does *anybody* want to stay at school for dinner?' I would ask, eating a phantom meal in exaggerated mime, and turning the hands of the cardboard clock to noon. Yet when the register had been sent in and the money checked, a dissatisfied customer would invariably appear saying he did/didn't want dinner, whichever was the more inconvenient, and just as I was probing his intentions a family of five would arrive for admission, all demanding to stay for the meal.

Saeed, the dinner monitor and a wizard at arithmetic, would stand breathing down my neck as I totted up

48

and converted. 'Wrong! Wrong! Mistake!' he would roar, pointing an accusing finger at my total.

'Bring the magic bottle,' I would say to little Jagindro, who squeaked with excitement as she watched the ink eradicator blotting out an error from the accounts. But the moment of truth came one Monday morning when even Jagindro realised that Miss was, in fact, no sorcerer.

'It's not magic!' she twittered. 'Miss has made a mistake.'

If the children who stayed for dinner created problems, those who did not could be an even greater worry. In most families the main meal of the day was eaten in the evenings, and some did not even bother to go home at twelve o'clock. They hastened instead to Woolworths, where a special doorman had to be posted to prevent them from joy-riding on the escalator. Though no one approved of these children either wandering the streets or going without food and drink at midday, there was little that could be done, and they never seemed any the worse for their voluntary fast.

What's in a name?

Teachers unfamiliar with immigrant work assume, naturally enough, that language is the one great difficulty to be overcome, and that when teacher and taught understand each other, education can proceed on normal lines. The language problem is, however, quite the simplest and the most straightforward of those with which the head of a Special English Department has to deal, for many other matters, administrative, medical, social, jostle for attention, and tasks which in a normal school are merely routine can be involved and confusing.

If admissions could have been made monthly, or even every half-term, the burden of administration would have been eased, but since a child of compulsory school age requesting entry could not legally be turned away, we had to accept new arrivals on any day and at any time.

The intake always reached its peak in the summer months. In May, June and July, a time of year when an ordinary school admits only the occasional newcomer, we took in over ninety children, and in 1967 the wall graph on which entries were recorded vanished clean through the ceiling. On the first day of the September term another ninety-seven were queuing up on the doorstep, and in every week of the following school year five more, perhaps even ten or fifteen, had somehow to be squeezed in.

Boys outnumbered girls by six to one. When a father decided to bring his family to England he always gave preference to his sons, for whom an education was important, and who in two or three years' time would themselves be wage-earners. His daughters came later, as and when finances allowed.

Every week a succession of fathers climbed the stairs to my room, followed by their solemn, wide-eyed children, and sometimes mother came too, walking a few paces behind her husband and carrying the baby, or with a black-haired toddler clinging to her coat. Older boys were often brought by an uncle and stood deferentially in the background in smart new suits and shiny shoes.

In halting English, father or uncle would try to give me the information I asked for, but mother, understanding only Punjabi, invariably remained silent. Straining desperately to understand, I would ask to see the passport and endeavour to fit the names written on it to the children standing so shyly before me.

Asian names proved surprisingly easy to pronounce, and most of them, we found, were directly connected with religion. Almost all our early pupils were Indian by birth and Sikh by religion. Sikhism was a breakaway from the old Hindu faith and a repudiation of its accompanying caste system. To be a Hindu had meant

51

that a man was born into a certain section of society, a station in life in which he was fated to remain for ever. He had a caste name which proclaimed his status to the world. He must marry within that caste and his children would be born into it. He could hope for no advancement, no progress, no escape.

We saw the system in action when we admitted a Brahmin, a member of the highest, or priestly caste. His superiority was accepted at once and without question by the class, who brought him his milk, carried his books, sharpened his pencils and obeyed his every whim and word.

To the ten great gurus, the teachers and leaders of the Sikhs, the caste system was anathema. Influenced by their Muslim neighbours they believed that men were born equal and that all were brothers. In their holy books and in their prayers they proclaimed the kinship of all mankind under one God. In order to emphasise this belief, so central to their faith, the last and most famous of the gurus, Gobind Singh, decreed that the Sikhs must put away their tell-tale caste name and take instead another indicative only of sex and religion. All male Sikhs were to be called Singh, meaning a lion, and all females Kaur, a charming compliment to womanhood, since some believe that the word originally meant a princess.

After some initial confusion we realised that this method of nomenclature was simplicity itself. Balbir Singh, for instance, was a male Sikh, but was not necessarily related to Jit Singh. Balbiro Kaur and Jit Kaur were female Sikhs, but their families might be completely unconnected. Their father could be Keval Singh and their mother Manjit Kaur, for a woman did not change her name on marriage and children did not take their father's name. If they did remember their old family name, and some of them did, we used it, but more often than not it had been genuinely forgotten.

Either the supply of Indian first names was limited, or families were unenterprising in their choice, for there were always squads of children with exactly the same name, which added considerably to our difficulties. Jasbinders, Jaswinders, Jasbirs and Jaswants proliferated, and a trio of eager voices answered every question addressed to Banso. Like Homer and the Welsh before us, we resorted to epithets, and just as they had their swift-footed Achilles, their Jones the Fish and Morgan the Meat, we had our Worried Banso and Laughing Banso, our Fat Banso and Thin Banso, our Tidy and Scruffy Amriks.

Then there were families who, inexplicably, gave all their children the same name. Satnam Singh I had a brother Satnam Singh II, and a sister Satnam Kaur.

Many of the commonest first names were sexless, and could be given indiscriminately to boys or girls. That much we had established, but shorn of their Singhs and Kaurs, who could distinguish male from female?

No newcomer was admitted until the family passport had been produced, but the name on this document did not always tally with that of the child before me. Father had simply changed his mind at the last moment and decided to bring number two son instead of number one as originally planned, or perhaps even a nephew.

Since in the Punjab a child's name was not always

officially registered at birth, it could even go for years without one, or at least without a proper one. A pet name, an endearment, a diminutive, Gudi perhaps, or Baby or Pami sufficed, but when the family, having decided to emigrate, applied for a passport, the issuing official was adamant. No Gudis or Pamis for him! It was proper names or nothing.

'Very well, then!' the father might say indifferently. 'Choose the names yourself!' So the passport officer wrote down the first names that came into his head, and they were instantly forgotten by the family. Many of our children had been 'christened' in this haphazard way, and protested loudly when we persistently addressed them by the names under which they had been admitted, but of which they had never even heard.

Once in England, the father might then decide to make a further change and to give the child a real name of his own choosing, which was duly and officially entered upon the passport.

The fact that a small child's name was so unimportant never ceased to surprise us. Real names, amongst village children at least, were apparently given when infancy with all its uncertainties was safely left behind, pet names sufficing until adolescence or sometimes until marriage. Could this be, we wondered, because of the high infant mortality rate in Asia? Was there no point in giving a name to a child who might not survive?

When Gudi was born, her uncle ran to the headman of the village to register the birth. 'A gudi has been born!' he cried excitedly. A gudi, in Punjabi, is a tiny baby, a little doll, so Gudi she became and Gudi she remained, even on her passport, until she was fifteen and ready to leave her English secondary school, when she was at last given a real name, since 'little doll' was no longer appropriate to the tall athletic girl she had grown to be.

The Indian children born in towns, and they were comparatively few, had, however, been named with due formality according to Sikh custom and taken to the temple when they were a few weeks old. There, in the presence of parents and relatives, the religious leader had opened the *Granth Sahib*, the holy book of the Sikhs, at random and read out the first word on the page thus revealed. The child was then given a name beginning with the same letter.

The Pakistanis were Muslims and bore names closely associated with the history of their faith. Every boy had at least two names, but it was important to remember that the second of these in no way corresponded to a western surname. Family names were, in fact, extremely rare. One of the chosen two was frequently that of the Prophet himself, Mohammed, but it was an indication of religion rather than a name to be used, and Mohammed Ali was known as Ali, Mohammed Rafik as Rafik.

Many boys had at least one name chosen from the ninety-nine attributes of God, and their other names might be those of the Prophet or his family, Ali, his beloved cousin, Abbas, his uncle, or Hassan and Hussein, two of his grandsons. Some, as in the Christian world, bore the names of saints and martyrs, of converts to Islam, or prophets and warriors of the faith, and Saeed and Akhbar, Manzoor and Idris, were soon as familiar to us as John and Peter, Michael and George.

The order in which the names were written was

vitally important, since Mohammed Bashir was not the same boy as Bashir Mohammed. The permutations of the commonest Muslim names seemed unending. At one time and on one register there were Mohammed Latif and Latif Mohammed, Abdul Latif and Latif Abdul, as well as Mohammed Akram, Mohammed Aslam and a bewildering row of Naeems, Naseems and Nasreens.

Muslim girls might have only one name, which was a relief. Where a second existed, it was probably Bibi, or less frequently Akhtar, Begum or Parveen. Some names were so beautiful that they almost sang themselves into the memory. Sushila, Shamuna, Shahida, Shafreen . . . My register was like a page from the *Arabian Nights*.

If teachers were puzzled by all this, bureaucracy was shattered. SURNAME their forms demanded uncompromisingly, and surnames there had to be. In spite of warnings of impending muddle, the Education Office set about creating them by reversing the order of the applicant's names. All went well with the Sikhs. Keval Singh entered as Singh Keval confused no one, but with the Muslims chaos set in. The Mohammed Latifs were continually being mistaken for the Latif Mohammeds, Sattar Mohammed turned up at a medical intended for Mohammed Sattar, and Akhtar Mohammed was given an injection destined for the veins of Mohammed Akhtar.

To turn Mohammed into a surname was, as we frequently pointed out, not only incorrect but ludicrous, since Mohammed Akram could have a father called Niaz Ali and a brother Abdul Ghafar, whilst our other Mohammeds were no relation to him at all except as brothers under the one God. Our advice, though well-meant, went unheeded, and even Bibi, simply a polite form of address for a Muslim girl, was treated as a surname, whilst Muslim and Sikh alike were allotted 'Christian' names. A few of our Indians were in fact Christians, with names which were balm to the office.

Addresses, though less confusing, could still be difficult to make out, for a garbled pronunciation, or even a shift of emphasis from one syllable to another, could turn a familiar place name into a mystery.

'Your address, please!' I would say to the father as I noted details of the passport, then listen intently for sounds which might conceivably resemble the name of a street or terrace in the neighbourhood.

'Mouse Treat,' he would say confidently.

'Mouse Treat?' I would echo, making a mental tour of the district.

'Yes, yes! Number four, Mouse Treat. O.K?'

'Oh! *Mount* Street?'

'Yes, yes! Like I tell you! Mouse Treat.'

The infant from Hell Top was obviously from Hill Top, and Kink's Place was Kirk's Place, but The Third Backside was a poser. It turned out to be a back to back house on the main road.

We had no guarantee that an address once given was permanent, for the children of brothers were more or less interchangeable, and a boy or girl would live happily for a time with an uncle, then move on to grandparents. Cousins were therefore considered as brothers and always asserted that they were so.

'Who is he?' I would ask.

'He is my brother. My father's brother's boy.'

57

There is, in fact, no one word for cousin in Punjabi, which accounts for some, at least, of the misunderstandings with which immigration officers have to deal at ports of entry.

The recording of name and address was child's play compared with what was to follow. Taking a deep breath, I proceeded to the 64,000 rupee question.

'Date of birth?' I would ask hopefully, pen poised for action.

'Born 1954. Him twellav!' said the father with a conviction I could hardly share, for the small boy hiding timidly behind his mother's coat could scarcely be more than eight. A glance at the passport confirmed his statement, but as we knew from experience, a date of birth given on a passport was not necessarily correct. Once again I had to face the recurring problem of a child's true age, which was frequently difficult, often impossible, to determine.

Registration of births in the Punjab was not enforced by law. In the past, especially in the country areas from which most of our children came, the headman of the village might be asked to register the birth when next he visited the town, but if his bicycle happened to be out of order, or the roads had been made impassable by floods, his trip might be indefinitely postponed. Either the matter was not followed up, or his memory being shaky, he could hazard only a guess at the details. In recent years, however, registration in the villages has become more systematic and is undertaken by lady health visitors whose efforts may, perhaps, make it easier for teachers and officials to determine the exact age of future immigrants.

Since birth dates were unimportant to Sikh and

Muslim alike, and since neither celebrated birthdays, there was no family record to supplement the lack of official documentary evidence. In a village community where many parents were illiterate there was nothing corresponding to the entries in the family Bible, and certainly nothing to compare with the parish registers which preserved the facts in the days before registration became compulsory in England.

When father decided to emigrate, the information was, however, required for the family passport. Face to face with an official who demanded the exact natal day of each of their three or six or even eight children, a quick approximation was the best the parents could manage. Often they honestly could not remember, so the passport official guessed, and sometimes the guesses were wild indeed. Mother, eager to be helpful, might proffer the information that 'he was born at the time of the river flood,' and the harassed functionary would date the child from a flood of his own, and not from the one in question.

So it came that we had Akhtar, officially eleven, but with a 40in chest and 5ft 8in tall, with a deep baritone voice and the beginnings of a moustache. Fully developed young women, obviously of marriageable age, could be anything from nine to twelve, and one had all her wisdom teeth, which was more than could be said for the clinic nurse who was assisting at her medical examination.

At the other end of the scale were tiny tots legally recorded as eight or even eleven, but whose whole physique, mode of play and general behaviour were those of a child of four, or even three, yet since they were officially of school age they had to be admitted.

Adorable though they were, they could be a problem. They could not blow their noses, could hardly climb on to a chair, even of the infant variety, and preferred to pursue their education from underneath it, attracting teacher's attention by tweaking her ankle as she passed. Tiny Tif, whose walk was still a swaying trot, felt safer in the kneehole of her desk. His companion, showing more initiative, posted a term's supply of pencils through a crack in the floorboards. It was all very funny until one realised that according to their passports some of these children should be sitting for the eleven-plus, and that one, at least, should be at a secondary school.

Obviously such cases were the exception rather than the rule, and it was important to bear in mind that some children who looked younger than their official age were undersized because of malnutrition. Even a casual visitor to the clinic could not fail to notice that Indian and Pakistani babies born in this country were much bigger and sturdier than those born in Asia, for English ante-natal care and an improved standard of living had made an unmistakable difference.

When the discrepancy between age and physique seemed quite inexplicable, parents were pressed for more precise information. It was not, after all, very easy to accept that identical twins had arrived a year apart, or that two brothers had appeared within three months of each other. Since mother and father spoke little or no English the interview took strange turns.

'You see,' said a father when asked why a child of six was bigger and stronger than a brother of eleven, 'when he was born he was already ten months old.'

Mother could sometimes tell us that the birth was

on a Friday or a Monday, but little else, and given her limited English and my less than sketchy Punjabi, even this was an achievement. One told me mournfully that when the child was born, the tree in her garden was 'so high,' but she didn't know how high it was now.

The blank birthdates might perhaps be supplied by helpful Sikh fathers in the form of a Punjabi date, but it was a date on a Sikh calendar, and even our Sikh teachers could not convert it into Gregorian time.

Once, after I had worked my way laboriously through a family passport, the father produced a second brood almost identical in age to the first. Two children born in one year? It was a possibility—once! But even in the most fertile circles it could hardly have happened five times. The second batch, I discovered, were the children of his second wife, but since neither wife could produce a marriage certificate, there was no real guarantee that the second family was his at all. But then no one could disprove it either.

When the credibility gap was too great, the school doctor examined the child in question, and from the bone structure, dentition and general physique decided whether it was more infant than junior, or more junior than senior. The obvious misfits could then be placed in the group most suited to their development. Where the doctor himself had doubts, the child was X-rayed at the hospital, where a more detailed assessment could be made. Such estimates could never be exact, but they were for use only within the education system and were needed merely as a guide to class grouping. A boy was free to leave school if his passport gave his age as fifteen. If, on the other hand, he had simply been estimated as fifteen, but was thirteen on his passport, he was compelled to remain.

For the Youth Employment Officer the passport was the immigrant's only legal document, unless of course he had a genuine birth certificate which only a few possessed. If according to his passport a boy was of compulsory school age, he could not be employed. Sometimes a boy who had been admitted as a junior on his mother's passport would apply for a passport of his own a year or two later and emerge with an entirely different date of birth, one which made him several years older, eligible to leave school and go to work.

Since admission day was one of the few occasions, often indeed the only one, on which we ever saw the parents, it was essential to find out as much as possible about the family. Above all we begged them to escort their youngest children to school in the morning and to collect them at four o'clock, at least for the first few days, pointing out that English mothers almost without exception arranged to bring and fetch their five-year-olds in the early weeks of their school life.

For these village-bred children, the walk home was full of danger, but only rarely could parents be made to see this, and the majority were reluctant to accept their responsibility. Again and again we were left with weeping infants who at four o'clock, or even at five, still waited in vain for an escort. Willing staff, or Education Welfare Officers ran them home in their cars, cheerfully at first, but with growing impatience when the same pathetic children were left abandoned time after time.

Sometimes youngsters who had escaped our vigilance would set out alone, to be instantly lost in the maze of unfamiliar streets through which they wandered help-less and in tears. By eight or nine in the evening they might still not have been traced, and that all were eventually retrieved without disaster was a tribute to the patient police and to the kindly townspeople who, often at great inconvenience to themselves, found out where they lived, or brought them back to school, or rang up the headmaster for help. The answer to the question 'Where do you live?' was one of the first phrases taught to every child, but in moments of panic the well-rehearsed phrases fled, or emerged in a form so garbled that strangers not tuned in to Asian voices could make nothing of them at all.

At the root of every such problem was a mother terrified of going out alone. It was impossible not to be sorry for her, but on our more harassed days we might have been forgiven for thinking that she could perhaps have made the effort to learn the route from her husband, if only for the sake of the children.

Fortunately the difficulty arose only with mothers new to the country. By the time their second child had reached school age they were moving about the town with growing confidence, whilst those who had borne most of their children in England brought and collected them without any prompting from us.

Never having been to a school before, many parents were fascinated by what they saw there. The play-things, the number apparatus, the bright books, opened up a whole new world, and they would sit at the low tables absorbed in play, exclaiming with delight when jigsaws fitted together and building bricks interlocked to make a wall. In fact we were hard put to it to get rid of them, but their enjoyment was so real, their pleasure so apparent, that it seemed heartless to tear them away. They began to collect their children earlier and earlier, and we found ourselves telling the last story of the day to a mixed class of mothers and infants, with the odd father lurking in the Wendy House pretending not to listen, but as enraptured by Cinderella as his six-year-old daughter. 'My daddy say Shindoella a very good stoory,' she would report next day.

Before immigration became a national issue, the health hazards it might bring were thought of, if at all, as a minor problem. In our early days no special arrangements were made for the medical examination of incoming children, and they took their turn with the rest of the school, waiting for the doctor's next routine visit, which might not be for several months. There seemed no cause for alarm.

The first stirrings of disquiet came with the smallpox epidemic of 1961. There was no case in the town and no evidence whatever that the disease had been brought to the West Riding by an immigrant, but though the scare soon died down, a residue of unease remained. The possibility that we might unwittingly admit an infected child no longer appeared remote, and the infection might well be not smallpox but tuberculosis, to which Asian immigrants seem especially prone. It was suggested to the Authority that every newcomer should be medically examined as soon as possible after entry, but since our fears had so far proved groundless, and such a scheme would place further burdens on medical and welfare staff already hard-pressed, no action was taken.

Two years later, it happened. Khalid was a tall, thin boy of thirteen. His face was drawn and weary and he was unusually listless. Occasionally he would put his head on the desk and fall fast asleep. He had no cough and did not appear to be ill. There was nothing odd about his condition, for lassitude and withdrawal were among the commonest symptoms of culture shock from which adolescent boys sometimes suffered severely, but when after a month he showed no sign of recovery his father took him to the doctor. He was found to be in an advanced and highly infectious stage of tuberculosis.

With the consent of parents, who took the news with admirable good sense, every child in the school was given a Heaf skin test, and teachers, caretakers, kitchen and cleaning staff were X-rayed, but no second case came to light.

Worrying and potentially dangerous though the incident was, it had one salutary effect. From then on every Asian child was skin-tested as soon as possible after arrival. A positive reaction, and there were always a few, did not necessarily mean that the child was infected, but that at some time it may have been in contact with tuberculosis or with one of several other diseases. Even so, every suspect was sent for X-ray and the family kept under supervision.

In our experience there were very few children who had actually brought tuberculosis into the country. At very rare intervals when the disease recurred, the boys and girls affected had in every case been living in England for two or three years and had been tested and cleared whilst with us. An innate tendency to the disease, which in the warmth and sunshine of their homeland would probably have remained dormant, had been aggravated by a cold, damp climate, by overcrowded living conditions in old, substandard houses, and by contact with infected adults for whom, at that time, there might have been no health check at the port of entry.

We left nothing to chance. Children born in England or who had moved in from another town were examined as carefully as new arrivals and sometimes proved positive. It was always possible that a child could be reinfected from its parents, and our precautions had to be strict in order to protect not only the immigrant children themselves but the English pupils in our own school, and in those to which the Asian children would eventually be transferred. Not one left us without being given the BCG injection, the standard protection against the disease.

No medicals, tests or injections were carried out without the written consent of parents who, often illiterate, were bewildered by the many forms which their sons and daughters were continually waving before them, and never knew for certain whether they were booking for a pantomime, ordering hyacinths or accepting an invitation to a jumble sale. It was difficult enough, even with an interpreter, to get the message across to the children.

'Take this home', we would say, 'and ask daddy to write his name *here*. Bring it back tomorrow.'

'Jikshuns?' they would enquire nervously. 'Don't like!'

In six years only one parent refused to allow his son to receive either a BCG or a medical examination, but his obstruction only served to emphasise the goodwill and co-operation of the rest, who fulfilled our requirements readily and realised that their children's health was a matter of importance and concern.

The school Medical Officer became as much a feature of our lives as shalwar and turbans, for in addition to the Heaf test our charges were given all the other inoculations they had missed in early childhood. 'Jikshuns!' the word went round whenever he appeared, and the sight of his tall figure sent a ripple of apprehension through the ranks. He had an intuitive understanding of children, reassuring the panic-stricken and dealing patiently with the shy and the reticent, particularly with the older Muslim girls for whom it was a terrifying ordeal to be examined by a man. A nurse, of course, was always with him, but if they were very frightened I, too, would stay in the room, perhaps holding their hand or patting them now and then on the shoulder, assuring them in my skimpy Punjabi that all was well.

The chest examination was a tricky procedure and considerable sleight of hand was needed if stethoscope and patient were ever to be brought together. Nurse was a hearty West Indian, with no time to spare for Muslim inhibitions. 'Vest up!' she would say briskly, whipping it smartly into position. The terrified girl immediately pulled it down again, and so the battle went on, with the vest flicking up and down like a roller blind, and the doctor enjoying the comedy and waiting, stethoscope at the ready, for the appropriate site to be revealed. Nurse usually won—in the end!

She was equally firm with reluctant injectees. 'If they have a consent form,' I told her one day, 'don't take any notice of what they say. Just give them the injection.' She did exactly that. When Resham Singh skipped down from the juniors with a consent form for his infant brother, he was thrust into the queue, in spite of his frantic claim that he had already been done. It was a relief to learn that no harm could come from a second dosage.

Many of the little ones had a shuddering dread of 'jikshuns' and came to associate me with the loathed operation. As soon as I entered a room and called a name, there would be screams and moans, even when I was merely collecting them for a film show.

An outbreak of scabies in local schools brought the doctor yet again, but this time it was to be only a brief encounter, no skin-tests, no 'jikshuns', just a fleeting glance at arms and chests. He installed himself at the far end of the library, whilst nurse stood ready to steer the line of children along the wall, behind the screen and out again. With seniors and juniors the plan worked perfectly. The infants disorganised it in seconds. Asked simply to lift up their shirts, the boys concluded that this was Music and Movement and began to strip off in all directions, the girls meekly following their lead. Braces clattered through the air, shalwar lay everywhere in shapeless heaps, organdie and muslin came to rest like tired meringues on library tables. The room was full of naked infants, screeching as they looked in vain for shorts and knickers.

'No! No!' cried their frantic Miss, pulling up trousers as fast as they were taking them down, but they went on with their striptease. The column began to move around the screen. Miss fielded the first to emerge and tried desperately to find their clothes.

Meanwhile a circular movement had developed among the patients, and since to the uninitiated, Asian children all look alike, the doctor continued to scrutinise arms and bosoms he had already inspected several

68

times before. 'This is a big class,' I heard him say to nurse. It was only when tiny Tif, so very much smaller than the rest, went trotting round the screen for his third visitation, that light began to dawn. 'But I've seen this little chap twice before,' said the doctor, and the session ended in helpless laughter as the performing troupe was led away. The doctor had enjoyed himself. This school, he declared, was different, and he asked that he might be allowed to conduct all our medicals in future. For once we were appreciated.

Most of the children were healthy, if a little under-sized and undernourished. Some had 'spocks,' which generally turned out to be impetigo, and some had trachoma, but serious illness was rare, and attendance figures in the department were uniformly high, above the average for the main school. The resilience and toughness which had enabled these youngsters to adapt so quickly seemed to give them a natural immunity from minor childish ailments, and even head colds were not very common.

Dental trouble in newcomers was rare. The brilliantly white and even teeth which made their smiles so attractive were as yet unspoiled by sweets and chocolates, but alas! not for long. The bubble-gum machine at the corner shop was continually in action, though having secured their pennyworth they were not quite sure what to do with it. Finding that it could not be swallowed and would not chew away, they pulled it out for examination, tried to put it in their pockets, then to throw it away, and ended up with lumps stuck to their fingers, suits, shirts and faces, and rubbery strings festooning their entire person. Lollipops and gob-stoppers soon wrought havoc too. 'Miss! My tooth is hurting!' became a familiar cry, and Mossadeq followed me everywhere whimpering, 'Miss! My tooth is outing!' and waggling a stump to prove his point.

An unfortunate few had tragic physical deformities, tragic because they could have been prevented if correct medical aid had been given in the first place. One boy had a foot so twisted that only the side of his big toe touched the ground and he limped badly. The leg ligaments had been cut by a ploughshare when he was small and had been most inexpertly repaired, but after orthopaedic treatment his walk was much improved.

A girl of thirteen had an unrepaired cleft palate which caused even her Punjabi speech to be unintelligible. Within six weeks of coming to England she had undergone the operation which should have been performed in babyhood, and after hours of patient tuition from the speech therapist she soon learnt to speak correctly. One of her eyes, too, was seriously defective. We kept her until glasses were fitted and then sent out a remarkably confident little girl.

There was a fairly high incidence of marginal deafness not always easy to detect in a newcomer. The inattention and heedlessness which quickly betray its presence to a trained teacher could be, and often were, due to lack of English or to psychological upheaval. Even the simple hearing test given by the audiologist did not always resolve the doubt, since children already in a state of shock were too confused to obey instructions, even when they had been simply and clearly explained by an interpreter. The headphones, the mysterious box, were yet another menacing feature of this frightening new world and there was no guarantee

70

that the child's responses had not been made at random.

Those severely handicapped by their disability were, of course, sent to a special school and often made remarkable progress, though since tuition in speech and lip-reading was based on English, the training, valuable though it was, could not always facilitate the child's communication with Punjabi-speaking parents and relatives. It might actually create a psychological barrier between them.

As with orthopaedic defects, much of this deafness was due to lack of care in infancy and childhood, for wax, boils, chronic suppuration, inflammation of the middle ear were not regarded as illnesses but simply as minor and inescapable hazards of childhood, too trivial to require the attentions of a doctor.

One teenage Sikh presented himself for examination still wearing his turban. Although he had been in school for several weeks he had never once removed it and no pressure had been put on him to do so.

'It's odd,' I said to the doctor, 'but he never makes any move to take it off.'

'Not odd at all,' he reported a few minutes later. 'The boy has no ears. Just a vestigial lobe, and he'll have to have surgery if he's ever to hear properly.'

The father who brought him for admission had not even thought the matter worth mentioning.

The work of the department, already seriously disturbed by these medical sessions, was still further interrupted by a stream of visitors. As Commonwealth immigration began to affect other towns, neighbouring authorities took a growing interest in our work. Cars full of their HMIs, head teachers and students, came bouncing down our cobbled street, picking their way among the broken bottles and battered prams, avoiding with difficulty the groups of toddlers, white, black and brown, who ran, sat, shrieked and wept in cowboy hats or nothing at all.

Our guests came for a variety of reasons and with a multitude of differing theories, but all were fascinated by what they found, sensitive to the atmosphere of warmth, of gaiety and vitality which made this school such a special place. Some, about to set up their own immigrant centres, wanted advice on administration and equipment, instruction in method, information about social problems and difficulties. Others were interested in the teaching of English as a second language preparatory to taking posts abroad, often in India or Pakistan, whilst the more academic sought material for their theses and data for their theories.

. Our protégés were always eager to show off their English, but were embarrassingly frank in their comments. 'Look!' they exclaimed when an eminent but balding HMI walked in. 'He has no middle hair!' Once they had the shock of their lives. The story of Hansel and Gretel, to which they had listened entranced, was just drawing to its close when in walked a lady of uncertain years, with iron grey hair and a long thin face. 'A witch! A witch!' they yelled, and my most reliable boy was so startled that he fell off his chair and was resuscitated in the midst of chaos. The witch turned out to be charming. When she showed the class a photograph of her mother they subsided into a reverential silence. That anyone so ancient should have a mother was beyond their comprehension.

Every visitor saw not only the Special English classes

with their graded language work, but the normal school as well, for there, as I always emphasised, the real work of integration was done. Again and again I marvelled at the patience and goodwill of the staff who laboured with these integrated, unstreamed classes. Already coping with children of the widest imaginable ability range, they never failed to welcome in another, and yet another, immigrant child who was ready to leave the department. And 'ready' never meant that the boy or girl could slip easily and at once into the work and routine of a junior group. It meant rather 'needing special attention, sympathy and understanding' from teachers on whom the rest of the class made exacting demands, and who in being fair to immigrant and non-immigrant alike were obliged to divide their loyalties and their time. It should be recorded to their credit that they rarely failed, and it was their care and encouragement which enabled our children to take the last vital step towards assimilation.

From the very first, the department had no difficulty in recruiting staff. All were volunteers and all were enthusiastic about the new venture, bringing to it a willingness to experiment and a fluidity of approach which were essential to its success. We were a mixed crowd, but each had a distinctive contribution to make. Some were teachers of several years standing who had welcomed this chance to break new ground though they had no previous experience of language work. Some were sociologists who had not taught before but were deeply interested in the children, as well as in their background and in the wider aspects of immigration. Others were trained linguists who had never before taught children of primary age.

When the first Asian teachers were appointed we had at last interpreters who could explain instructions and communicate with parents. As numbers increased, more and more Indian and Pakistani staff joined us and were attached to the beginners' classes, where their assistance was most needed. Speaking between them Hindi, Urdu and Punjabi, they could help the children to settle down, train them in road safety and the use of the toilet, reassure them about food, interpret and often solve their worries.

These Asian colleagues of ours had adjustment problems too. Accustomed in their own education to strict discipline and to formal methods of teaching, they were shocked by the lively activity methods of an English primary school, and by the easy, casual relationship between teacher and taught. Though too polite to say so, they must often have thought we were crazy, and bad disciplinarians into the bargain. It took some time to convince them that the free modern methods wholly alien to their academic tradition could, and did, produce results, but with goodwill on both sides, initial misunderstandings could generally be cleared away and happy associations formed.

Since children fresh from the Punjab were continually streaming in, classes were never stable for long. Every teacher of every class knew that every week would bring two or three new arrivals all of whom would have to be taught from the beginning. This in itself was a strain, but more discouraging still was the fact that when a classroom was filled to capacity, a group, and it was always the top group, had to be moved up or moved out. The children who knew their way about the school, knew the names of the staff and could take messages, those who could cope with keys and cupboards, preside over the milk and be relied on to do the routine jobs, were always the first to go, leaving Miss or Sir to start again at the beginning, working from one term to the next within the narrowest of limits, teaching *ad nauseam* the same elementary phrases, the same basic topics, but denied the satisfaction of seeing their pupils make any but the most rudimentary progress. Even our Asian colleagues, who could vary the monotony by teaching in Punjabi, found the work repetitive and exhausting.

The steadily rising numbers posed a recurring problem for the Authority which, in the course of a single year and for several years in succession, found a whole schoolful of children deposited on its doorstep. Plans to meet the emergency had to be fluid, since it was impossible to forecast with any degree of accuracy how many would be arriving at any given time. Somewhere, somehow, classrooms had to be found to accommodate them, and teachers willing and able to cope with children who, for a while at least, would not understand a word that was said.

Every Education Authority is called on to cater for the occasional inexplicable bulge. Our trouble was not one bulge, but bulges all the time and all over the place. Our Authority faced the problems resolutely and faced them early. Others in a similar situation might have put forward different ideas, advocated different solutions, but at least no child in our town walked the streets because no place could be found for it in school.

We teachers were not alone in our problems. Doctors and hospital staffs, health visitors, shop assistants, postal workers and local government officials, all found their lives complicated.

'You can't imagine,' said my doctor, 'what difficulties arise when a seven-year-old boy comes to the antenatal clinic to interpret for his mother.'

'All these blinking Singhs!' said my postman as he peered at a pile of airmail letters. 'They must be a big family!'

The officials whose difficulties most resembled our own were the Education Welfare Officers, and so great was the burden placed upon them that in 1965 one of their number was appointed as Special Duties Officer with responsibility for immigrant children, West Indian as well as Asian.

It was an exacting job but a vitally important one, since he was often our only link with parents and the home, and it called for special qualities of patience, sympathy and firmness, all of which he possessed in good measure. His work was infinitely varied. In addition to his routine duties of checking up on children who were absent for no known reason, he had to explain the purpose of the Special English scheme to a father who kept his child away because our school was not easily accessible from his home, to make it clear that older girls were not to be kept at home to mind the baby whilst mother went shopping, and that 9am meant 9am and not 10.30. If a boy was found lurking in Woolworths during school hours, or a small girl found lost and weeping in the street after five o'clock, it was up to him to winkle out the culprit or tuck the wanderer in his car and take her home.

There were times when he had to settle delicate issues involving matters of conscience and religion. A

76

particularly devout branch of Islam to which a number of our Pakistani families belonged, insisted that its boys should attend Friday afternoon prayers at the mosque. The importance of this act of worship had been clearly laid down by their spiritual leaders and it was not easy to persuade fanatical fathers to send their sons to school instead, and to convince them that here in England education had a legal priority.

His home visits were sometimes successful, sometimes not. In the beginning he found it difficult to gain entry because Asians were afraid and mistrustful of authority in any form. His loud knocking usually drew a male head to an upstairs window, and eventually the door would be unbarred, unbolted, unchained and finally unlocked by the father of the household clad sometimes in pyjamas sometimes in a dhoti, a kind of voluminous loincloth. Once inside and identified he was welcomed with genuine hospitality. The mother, hiding in the kitchen, would send out for biscuits, and soon he was being regaled with cups of hot, sweet, milky tea and custard creams. Afterwards he was given a fervent promise, almost always kept, that the absentee would return to school the very next day.

If, however, father was at work when he called, the task was more difficult, for most of the women would run giggling upstairs as soon as he knocked and peep out at him from behind the curtains, too frightened to open the door. When the boldest among them ventured to make their presence known, their complete lack of English made explanations almost impossible and all he could do was to repeat the name of the child he was seeking.

'You wait!' the lady of the house would cry, then off

she would rush to her neighbour, her return heralded by high-pitched chatter as two women arrived to cope with him. It being reasonable to assume that Number Two was more fluent in English than Number One, he began all over again and managed to establish beyond question that Number One was the mother of the child on his list; but when it came to discovering the reason for the child's absence from school he found himself in difficulties once more.

'You wait!' shrilled Number Two and vanished down a passageway to collect Number Three. By the time Numbers Four, Five and Six had arrived on the scene the poor man was surrounded by veiled Punjabi mothers, all arguing among themselves, each with a different interpretation of his simple query. It was at that point that he usually beat his retreat.

At one house, however, there were no such difficulties. Since the teenage daughter was hardly ever at school he was so frequent a visitor that no words were needed to explain his appearance on the doorstep. Whipping up her kameez with most uncharacteristic immodesty, the mother would point to an impressive scar across her large brown tum. 'Prition!' she would explain with a disarming smile. Even the most cursory glance showed the embarrassed man that the operation was by no means recent and that the scar was a veteran, but it was still hard to make her understand that an illness of many years ago was not sufficient reason to deprive her child of education.

As both he and his work became known to the immigrant community they began to realise that his concern for their children was deep and genuine. When they saw him driving lost children home, and arranging their transport to and from school, they began to have confidence in him. They overwhelmed him with hospitality. They rarely kept their children away without reason and the fact that the average attendance hardly ever fell below 94 per cent was a tribute, not only to the toughness of the young but to his patient endeavours to make parents understand that regular attendance was not only expected but was legally enforceable, and that the obligation was as binding upon girls as upon their brothers. In his three years of immigrant work not a single legal action had to be taken against Asian parents for failing to send their children to school.

Cases of neglect or ill-treatment were equally rare, and the few which occurred were the result not of wilful cruelty but of thoughtlessness. Occasionally a father would return to Pakistan or India leaving a son in the nominal care of an uncle or cousin who took only the sketchiest view of his responsibilities.

One such case was discovered because the boy's employer was breaking a local bylaw in using him for part-time work when he was under age. The lad had been left to live in one room in the purely theoretical care of a relative who spent months in another town, and since he had to fend for himself he was suffering from serious malnutrition. He washed his own clothes, cooked his own meals and earned money for food by delivering newspapers. His plight was discovered when the Welfare Officer made a routine check of newsagents and the boy was taken into care and placed in a children's home.

It is a common accusation that immigrants sponge on and abuse the welfare services, yet between 1964 and 1967 the Welfare Officer did not receive a single application for free meals, footwear or clothing for Indian or Pakistani children. It was at his insistence that the boys and girls from two families in real need should have free school meals and warm clothing. In both cases the father had died in England, leaving non-English speaking mothers to cope with families of six and three respectively, but even they, desperate though their plight was, would never have lodged an application if he had not sought them out.

Among so large an Asian school population there were, of course, children who needed special, or even remedial education, and who even in their own culture were backward, or slow learners, or were in some way mentally or physically handicapped. The Welfare Officer assisted in allocating them to their appropriate schools, some of which were in the borough, some far outside its boundaries, and was responsible for their transport. Some attended a special school for the deaf, others a centre for remedial teaching. A boy who suffered severely from asthma was sent to a residential school in the country and was taken and brought back at holiday times in the Welfare Officer's own car, a task which, though time-consuming, was as nothing compared with the initial difficulty of explaining to the father that the sick boy was being sent away for his own good and not as a punishment.

Like us, the Welfare Officer had begun by assuming that a child's age was correctly stated on the passport, which was after all a legal document. Like us, he soon became convinced that in a number of cases the birthdate was wrong. He began to be inundated with sworn affidavits signed with the thumbprints of grandfathers and great-grandparents, certifying that boys entering the country as eleven-year olds were actually seventeen, and so eligible for work. Some even produced brand-new passports with brand-new dates of birth. Welfare workers, as well as teachers, continually bemoaned the lack of genuine birth certificates, and ardently wished that there could be some way of verifying essential documents at ports of entry or exit.

From our special Education Welfare Officer we learnt much that was of value about the homes and backgrounds of our children, for he had unique opportunities of seeing them in their natural environment with their families, and not putting on a display for teacher's benefit.

Most of the homes were clean, though bare, with lino or scattered rugs covering the floor, and simple furniture often bought from the original owner of the house. There would be a table, some chairs, a settee, always a television set, and sometimes a bed in the corner as well. Mother often made her chupattis squatting on the floor in the old Indian style. That, in fact, was where she did most of her work, and it was impossible not to feel pity for her lot, living as she so often did in a dark basement.

On one of his house visits, he found a woman crouching on the floor unpicking the stitches of her sewing with her teeth. His first impulse was to show her how much more quickly the work could have been done with scissors, but he decided against it.

'But why?' I asked.

'Because it was giving her something to do,' he answered. 'With scissors she would have finished the job in five minutes.'

The homes of Asians long established in England, and of those born and brought up in towns were, in contrast, completely westernised, indistinguishable from those of middle-class English families. They had come to realise that in this cold country, carpets were essential for warmth and comfort in a way they had never been in their own hot and dusty land, and that modern gas and electric heating systems were not luxuries but necessities.

Education welfare work has its lighter side, and over a cup of tea in the staff-room our 'school policeman', as the children called him, would read us extracts from the 'excuse' letters which flowed into his office. Many of them, though purporting to come from parents, were suspiciously reminiscent of the products of our ex-pupils.

'I am sorry not to have the dinner money,' wrote one, 'but owing to the balancing of the budget, I am having a difficulty.'

One resourceful senior always wrote his own absence notes, and very charming they were too.

Dear sir,
I am sorry that I, a bonafied student in your class, was not present before half-time. I beg to relate that it was our Xchristmas day. I mean to say I had been to Church and was not anywhere else.

Yours anticipation,
Bashir.

The letters from educated parents were, of course, always well composed, written in a beautiful hand and grammatically correct. The formal, courteous phrases, so typical of eastern good manners, were very flattering to our self-esteem until we found that they represented the usual form of address to anyone in authority.

> Dear Madam,
> With due respect and humble submission I beg to lay down the following few lines for your favourable and sympathetic attention.

We enjoyed being 'Most respected Madam,' 'Most Honoured Sir,' and even 'Your Excellency and Sir,' and were touched by the assurance that grateful parents would 'pray to the proprietor of the universe' for us.

How we began

'How ON earth do you begin?' visitors often wanted to know in the years that followed. It was a question I asked myself as I shepherded my flock to their class-room on that first historic morning, new to language teaching, new to the school and wondering what a lesson could consist of when neither teacher nor children could understand or be understood.

I need not have worried. 'Good morning!' they shrilled as I closed the door behind the last tiny straggler. 'Good morning! Good morning!' It was the only phrase they knew and they were determined to do it justice. The words came piping at me from every quarter, in every conceivable pitch and tone, not once but several times from every child, and went on coming. Gratifying though it was, this mass greeting would have to be curbed.

'One, two, three! Good morning!' I said with an all-embracing sweep of the hand to show that they were going to say it together. They smiled and nodded happily. My first attempt at communication had succeeded. Perhaps it was not going to be so difficult after all.

'One, two, three!' I counted again.

'Good morning!' they chanted in unison exactly as I had planned.

I was congratulating myself on this early triumph when, 'Good morning!' *soprano*. 'Good morning!' *bass*. 'Good morning!' *alto*. 'Good morning!' *falsetto*. 'Good morning!' *soprano* again. 'Good morning! Good morning!' We were still saying it when the bell rang for playtime.

We then began to say goodbye. It took a long time. As I stood by the door each child stopped in front of me and with hands together and a courteous inclination of the head said, 'Sat siri akal!'

'Goodbye!' I answered, wondering if I was expected to shake hands.

At the end of the line came my one little Muslim. 'Sat siri akal!' I said as he passed me. Having heard it seventeen times already I was proud of my pronunciation, but from his look of instant pain I knew at once that I had blundered.

'No, no, no, no, no!' he wailed. 'Indian sat siri akal! Pakistani a salaam a laykum!'

'A salaam a laykum!' I replied.

'No!' He was more troubled than ever. 'I a salaam a laykum. *You* wa laykum a salaam.'

'Wa laykum a salaam!' I repeated.

Even before he patted me on the head I knew that I had got it right.

Five minutes later as I came up the stairs barely fortified by a quick cup of coffee, they were queuing up to get in again. 'Good morning!' they said, beam-

85

ing a welcome as they saw me. 'Good morning! Good morning! Good morning!'

It seemed a long, long stretch to dinnertime. I felt as isolated as Robinson Crusoe, and even my simplest wants seemed impossible to achieve. The children understood none of my instructions, and every item of class routine involved me in exhausting pantomime. Problems piled up. The secretary had to wait for the dinner money. The Head had to wait for his stocklist. The children had to wait for their milk, and I, having filled the blackboard to overflowing, had to wait for a duster. Yet by four o'clock I had taught them something. 'Hello, Miss! Good morning! Goodbye!' they chanted as they escorted me to the bus. 'Hello, Miss! Good morning! Goodbye!'

Language was not the barrier I had expected it to be, for in a surprisingly short time we began to understand each other. Far more intractable were the problems posed by the extremely wide age range. Yet the mixture of juniors and teenagers had the spice of novelty and, as many a village schoolmistress has found, the older children gained much in stature from being responsible for the younger ones, helping them to hold a pencil and listening to the reading of those still struggling to decipher a strange new alphabet.

Ability was as varied as age, since highly intelligent children recently admitted knew less English than the plodders who had been in the class from the beginning. Group work, the obvious answer, was neither possible nor desirable for the whole of the school day, and difficult though it was to find material which would appeal to everyone, it was not impossible. There were actually topics, such as safety in the home, and fire precautions, highly necessary in an area where oil heaters were so prevalent, which came more alive when big and little could enact a scene together. Big Abdul could carry tiny Som Singh in perfect safety and with a masterly fireman's lift, from the window of our burning classroom, whilst the in-betweens dashed about shutting windows and phoning for the fire brigade.

Progress would certainly have been more rapid if the children could have joined an English class for creative activities in the afternoon, for isolated as they were in their special group, they heard the new language only in the playground, but such a scheme, which all agreed was ideal in theory, proved impossible in practice because of the sheer weight of numbers.

Lack of spoken English in the home was a further, and almost insuperable obstacle. A whole Punjabi-speaking weekend set some children back considerably, and each Monday morning had to be a 'tuning in' time when even the most able had to re-accustom themselves to the sounds and rhythms of English.

Admirers and critics of the Special English scheme, and there were both, took it for granted that we ourselves had learnt 'their language', and could not imagine how we could teach them effectively without it. In the first flush of enthusiasm, and not realising that most immigrants in the town spoke the Punjabi dialect of the Jullundur region, for which we had no textbook, we set out to learn Urdu, the official language of Pakistan.

We bought an Urdu grammar. The first chapter was not encouraging. Some sounds, said the author, especially the 'flapped and tapped' variety, took so long to prepare that you could hear them coming. The trouble was that in our case they never came at all.

With dismay we read of past presumptives, peculiar causals and postpositions. With despair we studied the exercises:

> The fly has fallen into the sherbet.
> This bull has a bad cough.
> Sinners keep on sinning.

When we reached 'the ant was squashed under the bed' we gave it up. There was nothing in this work which would help us to ask Ghulam why he had not brought his dinner money, to reassure a father that his daughter was not eating beef, or to bring home to Ahmad the fact that Saturdays and Sundays were holidays.

A knowledge of Hindi, the vernacular language of North India, would have been no more helpful, for both Hindi and Urdu were so politically loaded that proficiency in either would have aroused the Indian-Pakistani rivalries which lay just below the surface.

'Speak Indian!' commanded my young Sikhs and Hindus when I aired my single sentence of Urdu. It had been laboriously acquired and meant, I hoped, 'I'll smack your bottom.'

'Speak Pakistani!' shouted my Muslims when I ventured a phrase or two of Hindi.

'Speak English!' cried Meena, who had been brought up in Kenya and despised both factions. We decided to follow her advice.

Through constant association with the children, and by listening to our Asian colleagues we did however acquire a number of Punjabi words and Urdu phrases which, spoken briskly and unexpectedly, could command instant attention in an emergency and which sometimes slipped out in an English context. 'Jaldi! Jaldi!' I once urged my mother as she dawdled across a busy street. It was the peremptory command with which I propelled my crocodile over the zebra crossing on our visits to town, and it proved far more effective than, 'Do hurry up!'

Forced back upon English in the classroom, upon the direct method pure and simple, we managed surprisingly well. For the most part we got the meaning across by mime and gesture, by leaping and posturing, by acting, drawing and dramatising, but it was hard work, and both mentally and physically tiring. Sometimes we were defeated. When the office asked us to find out where each child had been born, we reached deadlock. We cuddled dolls, waved pictures of infants, of hospitals, of maternity wards, of new-born babies.

'Where was mummy when you came to her as a little baby?' we asked. 'Where were you when you were one day old?' Anxious to help, they listened politely, but their answers increased our desperation.

'In the house,' they said. 'At home. In the bed.'

In those early days there were no books to guide us. Simple readers for English children were useful only when the language was plain and natural. They were hard to find, for in most of those in common use it was stilted and unreal, using phrases which no Asian child, nor any other child for that matter, would use in everyday speech.

The subject matter was equally remote from life as they knew it, for in all of them the setting was impeccably middle-class. Well-dressed children, surrounded by toys, played with puppies and kittens in trim suburban gardens. They went for picnics in the car, or walked hand in hand against a background of delphiniums, and would not have recognised a chupatti if they had seen one.

Books printed in India were for use only in secondary schools, and were far too academic and advanced for juniors. Many were heavily moral, and staggeringly imperial.

> The monkey snatched off the adjutant's turban and ran up a tree.
> The captain ordered the artillery to fire from behind.
> The servant made tea for the Governor.

Even worse were English grammars brought by a few children from their villages. They taught strange passives, 'I am laughed. I shall have been laughed. I had been laughed,' and an even stranger terminology, 'I have the gleet. Thou hast the gleet. She has the gleet.'

The best buys were books produced for the Commonwealth countries. They were linguistically sound and usually colourful, but too culture-biased for our purpose, full of Nigerian children planting yams, Malaysian children playing on sampans, and Indian children shopping in street markets in Kenya, but we extracted all that was relevant to our needs. What we really wanted were books designed for young Asians in an English industrial setting.

When an English child learns its mother tongue, the first stage is one of listening and absorbing. Then comes imitation, experimentation, improvisation, and later, much later, the ability to read and write. I decided to follow this natural progression in my language teaching.

Classroom commands were perfect material for the listening time. 'Sit down!' I would say, putting each child bodily down on a chair. 'Stand up!' I said next, lifting each individual to its feet, and they stared in amazement at this mad Englishwoman who, having thrust them down, immediately heaved them up again. From this it was an easy step to, 'Open the door! Shut the door! Drink your milk! Put the bottle in the crate! Make a line!' and the drills were quickly understood and became an amusing game.

Children who had an ear for language soon began to imitate them and were allowed to be teacher and to give the commands themselves, and to our astonishment we found that those who were best at oral work were not necessarily the most intelligent.

Using the simple language of everyday things, we made the drills more complicated so that they grew out of each other like the ever-dividing branches of a tree, or were built one upon the other like bricks in a wall.

What's this?
It's a cardigan.
It's a big, blue cardigan.
Is this a cardigan?
Yes, it is.
Is this a cardigan?
No, it's not. It's a pullover.

Very soon a child of even limited ability was using correct sentences and speaking English with an accent far purer than that of the Yorkshire boys and girls with whom they played.

Everything had to be explained by visual means, by pictures or sketches on the blackboard, and later, when we acquired them, by flannelgraphs, cellographs and filmstrips. To vary the monotony, and to give my voice a rest, I sometimes used tape-recorded dialogues, which were valuable because the sentences never changed either in inflexion or phrasing as they were liable to do in ordinary conversation. 'Look at me!' brought an immediate response from the children when I spoke, but 'Watch me!' from the swimming instructress had no effect at all. In any recorded scene, my husband, revealing unsuspected histrionic talent, undertook to play the male roles. Unfortunately he had to play the extra female roles as well, and I had to explain away the decidedly bass boom of Mrs. Sugra Bibi by drawing and painting a very big, fat Punjabi woman who, I told them, had a very big, fat voice.

At first the children merely listened and watched as I made the figures on the flannelgraph act out the dialogue, but soon they began to repeat the words until they knew them by heart and could perform the scene in the classroom.

With a quick rearrangement of chairs it became the inside of a bus. Up and down the aisle paced the proud conductor, brandishing his roll of tickets made from perforated toilet paper and collecting fares from his passengers who had real pennies. Each child booked to its own street, for addresses could never be repeated too often, and the conductor had to read the list of streets from the blackboard in order to shout the fare stages.

Even in this simple play, the children began to improvise and, 'It's the wrong stop, you silly nit!' or similar gems, showed that language was being picked up in the playground as well as in the classroom. The naughty words, the swear words, seemed irresistible—and so easy to learn! In the end I was forced to recognise the need for an expletive of some kind, and consulted the experts in Junior 4. 'Blooming heck!' they advised unanimously, so into my scheme went blooming heck, for it was better than the four-letter word so constantly on the lips of even the most innocent, and which became such a feature of our lives that we were often tempted to correct its mispronunciation, or even worse, to use it ourselves.

Topic work gradually became more elaborate. From 'Conversation in the Bus,' we moved on to 'Lost in the Street,' and 'Shopping at the Market.' Improvised stalls were stocked with a wide range of goods, fruit, flowers, clothes, household articles, made from pictures cut out of magazines and mail order catalogues, and each mounted and labelled. The customers moved briskly around spending cardboard money with abandon and engaging in rustic badinage with the stall-holders, who thumped their price-lists in justification when accused of overcharging.

At the end of one bustling session, almost every coin in circulation had gravitated to the fruit-stall proprietor, Makhan Singh. I watched him closely. He did a roaring trade, for ignoring his price-list completely he was happily bargaining and auctioning with his clients, and doing a spot of money-lending on the quiet, exacting a crippling rate of interest from his fellow-stallholders. We had created a genuinely Indian market!

The same project, tried out with the infants, produced vastly different results, for whenever that wily

Pakistani Abdul Mohammed was given the job of shop-keeper, he promptly made a huge sign saying CLOSED, and sat behind the counter with his feet up.

When the market began to pall, we opened a café, with fancy paper tablecloths made in handwork classes, and neat, white caps for the waitresses, rustled up in sewing lessons. Though less useful than previous projects, for few of our children were likely to patronise an English café, it nevertheless produced much that was valuable in the way of vocabulary and idiom.

Both waitresses and customers had to be able to read the names written on the back of the cardboard food as well as the items on the menu, and had to add up the bills at the end. The waitresses were very efficient. They had to be, for angry clients kept waiting or served with the wrong dish made a constant uproar, banging their desks with their spoons, and when cook fluffed an order and sent up apple-pie instead of curry and rice, he was execrated in salty Punjabi and in broadest Yorkshire as well. There was thus a very strong motiva-tion to read. The general hubbub was increased by the cashier who, hating to be left for long without a bill to calculate, would constantly lean out of his cash-desk and urge the diners on with shrill cries of, 'Hurry up! 'Hurry up! Eat! Eat! Too long! Too long!'

'Going to the Doctor's' was not only the most amus-ing, but one of the most immediately helpful of our simulated scenes, for visits to the surgery were a rou-tine feature of the children's lives. The English winter brought on chest troubles, and mother was often expecting a baby. The word hospital was synonymous in their minds with giving birth, and when Miss returned to her infants after a spell in the infirmary their joy at seeing her again was tempered with genuine disappointment that her arms were empty. 'No baby?' they asked incredulously. 'You go to hospital and *no baby*?'

Whenever mother went to see the doctor, a child would go with her as interpreter, and do its valiant best to make some kind of dialogue possible between doctor and patient. If I could teach my class to give a clear and simple explanation of common symptoms, to say where a pain was felt, to understand instructions about medicines and tablets, about treatment, about staying in bed, then the lessons would have served a useful purpose.

Before beginning the dialogues we rehearsed the symptoms of every ailment likely to fall within their experience. Holding up a flashcard I HAVE TUMMY ACHE I read the phrase aloud, then writhed in what I hoped was a realistic attack of colic. The children too would repeat the sentence and double up and groan in gripes even more dramatic than my own. Soon I had only to hold up the flashcard and they were able to read the words and act appropriately without any help from me, whilst towards the end of the project most of them could write down the sentences as well.

Sometimes I tried to catch them out with a combination of symptoms. 'What's the matter with me?' I cried, sneezing and coughing, blowing my nose and croaking. 'I have a headache. I have a cold in my nose. I have a sore throat and my eyes are running. I feel very hot.'

'You have the 'flu,' was the answer I was hoping for.

'I think you're very nearly dead,' was the depressing diagnosis I was given.

The post office, like the surgery, was important in

95

their lives. As a project it involved far more than the simple dialogues required to buy stamps and postal orders. Airmail letter forms were continually needed, so too were postal orders, money orders and registered letters for the despatch of money to relatives in England and Asia.

At an improvised counter we deposited and withdrew money using our home-made bank books. We talked about the National Savings movement and every child in the class began to save. We learnt about licences for dogs and cars, for television and radio.

Letters were written and addressed, and postal charges to India had to be continually revised. With empty boxes and sugar paper and Sellotape the children made a variety of parcels with which to practise weighing and the filling in of customs forms.

Once, when business was booming and the classroom full of noise and bustle, a gentleman from Japan watched a customer painstakingly filling in his declaration for a parcel to India.

'Excuse me, young man,' said the earnest educationist, 'but what are you sending in that parcel?'

'Nothing!' replied Naeem, honest as the day. 'The parcel is empty.'

Which just goes to prove that even the most lifelike play is never as good as the real thing.

Everyone enjoyed 'The Railway Station.' The phone was used for enquiries about train times and the class learnt to read a simple timetable, to cope with the twenty-four-hour clock and to consult the destination board.

'Good morning,' said Balvinder. 'Can you tell me the times of trains to India?'

'We have no trains to India,' replied the flustered clerk, thumbing frantically through our home-made timetable. 'Go to Bradford instead.'

When they could ask for single, return and cheap day tickets, distinguish between first- and second-class compartments, read the platform signs, buy what they wanted from the coffee stall and the newspaper kiosk, they were taken to the real station as a reward for all their hard work. It was wonderful to see how much they had absorbed without realising that they were learning.

'There's the Left Luggage,' said Som Singh.

'Where's the Buffet?' asked Nirmal who was always hungry.

'And there's the Captain!' said Amrik as the station-master came to greet us. It was the only mistake they made.

Since so much had to be packed into so short a time, all these projects were based upon the children's immediate needs. Whenever they were able to stay with me longer, I went on to teach them about the public services.

After learning about the police, about how they could help, and how to get in touch with them, they were taken round the police station, where they were impressed, not so much by the majesty of the law, as by its sanitary arrangements. The provision of a lavatory, 'A *little* laverterry!' they exclaimed delightedly, in every cell, seemed to them such a luxury, such a gesture of goodwill towards the inmates, that it drove every other aspect of the visit clean out of their heads. Every time we passed 'the jail,' as they persisted in calling it, on our way to the swimming-baths, they would point and exclaim and tell any passer-by who would listen that there were 'many, many little laverterries,' and their individual booklets about the visit featured row upon row of what in that old-fashioned building, could hardly have been called modern conveniences.

In every possible way, topic work was linked with reality, both inside and outside school. Only 'The Seaside' remained a picture on the wall, until that, too, was brought to life by the trip to Whitby.

The children arrived long before the coach, looking clean and trim, the girls in new kameez and shalwar, the boys in neat suits and dazzling white shirts. Malkit Singh, born for big business, looked as if he had come straight from a board meeting, though his smart black briefcase contained, not plans for a merger, but chupattis for his lunch.

As they stood waiting in the yard we surveyed them fondly. It was wonderful to see the laughing, chattering group, and to feel their infectious happiness. 'Just look at Asghar!' I said, pointing to a seven-year-old who was jumping up and down. 'When you think what he was like this time last year!'

The transformation was, indeed, almost unbelievable. He had come to us neglected, down at heel, painfully thin, weighed down with responsibility for a minute, underfed young brother, and left to fend for them both in a household consisting entirely of men. His wizened face had been that of a weary old man, and everything about him, his unkempt appearance, his suspicion, his withdrawal, had cried aloud for affection and reassurance. He had been so deprived of possessions that when confronted with toys he collected them within the circle of his arms, growling like a dog if anyone came near. Now he was a laughing, happy child.

Yet, attractive though they were to us, with their gleaming black hair, their bright smiles, their dark eyes flashing with excitement, they aroused no such enthusiasm in the driver. 'Didn't know I'd got landed wi' a load o' blinking foreigners!' he said as he grumpily stowed the school milk in the boot.

Even before we had left the town boundaries, there were shrill calls for the sea. 'Where's the sea? Wherever is the sea?' they asked impatiently, but they were soon thrilled to see the fields and trees of the English countryside. 'It's the country!' some of them cried, remembering the class-room picture. 'Is *this* the country?' asked others, whilst, 'They are cows!' came from a solemn junior at the back, determined to use his language drills.

During the brief halt at York they hurled themselves upon the kiosk in the car-park. 'Crips, please! Crips! Crips! Crips!' they shouted at the girl behind the counter. (The Punjabi-speakers always had difficulty with their final *sps*.) The driver stepped nonchalantly to the head of the clamorous queue.

'They want a packet o' crisps,' he explained.

'Oh, that's it!' she said, and there was admiration in the glance she gave him. 'Do you understand their language then?'

'Oh, yes!' he replied modestly. 'You soon get used to it.'

He was definitely thawing.

We ate our lunch on the moors. Sheep wandered up for titbits and wandered away again looking thoughtful as they chewed hot curry and chupattis, for many of

99

the children had brought a complete Indian meal in the metal chupatti tins in which their fathers took lunch to work.

Soon the driver, elated by his linguistic triumph in the car park, began actually to enjoy our company.

'Why is he nearly stopping?' asked Surjit as we drove cautiously down the steep hill into Whitby.

'Because it's a very dangerous hill,' I told him. 'Look at the signs by the road. They say TAKE CARE, SLOW DOWN, and STEEP HILL. The driver is being very careful.'

Thirty-eight pairs of brown eyes stared admiringly at the navy blue back.

'Yes!' agreed the six front seats. 'He is a very good driver.'

'A very, very good driver!' echoed the passengers in the middle.

'A very, very, very good driver!' shouted the back rows, not to be outdone, and as the coach, still ringing with his praises, drew to a stop, he gave his delighted fans the boxer's victory salute. We might have been forgiven for thinking in our hearts that the victory was ours.

Leaving him to a well-earned rest, we marched through the Khyber Pass on to a cold and windy beach. The North Sea, a sullen grey, bore no resemblance to the stretch of sapphire on our wall picture. There was not a bikini in sight, and for that I was truly thankful. Here and there a few holidaymakers shivered in deck chairs, and most of them were so swathed in cardigans that not even the most delicate susceptibilities could be offended.

In spite of the cold the children were soon stripped

and into the sea. The smaller ones paddled, keeping their best clothes on and carrying their shoes in their hands. Little Aslam, though almost blue with cold, was determined to keep up with the rest and stood furiously sucking his iced lolly and whimpering as each icy wave washed over his ankles.

It was soon time to picnic. But where? The biting wind made the beach impossible, and only Malkit had an alternative to suggest. 'I want,' he said firmly, 'to go to an ottel.' An 'ottel' had figured prominently in our picture and he was determined to visit one. He was disgusted when we ended up in the bandstand. It had much to recommend it. Its sturdy roof gave us shelter, its low parapet gave us seats, and best of all, like a sheepfold it had only one narrow entrance, easily blocked with a rucksack.

With us inside it, the bandstand at once became a tourist attraction. Installed as we were in the middle of the promenade, we provided interest and light relief for the promenaders, and took their minds off the weather. As they watched the gay contingent and listened fascinated to the chatter, we realised, not for the first time, how intensely localised the immigrant problem was. Many of these holidaymakers, though living in Yorkshire towns not very distant from our own, were unfamiliar with the sight of boys in turbans and girls in Muslim dress, for immigration had in no way impinged upon their lives and was little more than a problem on the telly. All unconscious of their curiosity, our charges continued to munch their fruit and to deposit their cores and peel in Mr Piper's rucksack, an idea of theirs which, though it did credit to his anti-litter training lessons, he viewed without enthusiasm.

After a quick run round the amusement arcade, a last wild fling on the dodgems, and a final roll-call, we left for home. It was a hilarious journey. The driver, now completely won over, turned his cap the wrong way round and egged on his engine with an imaginary whip every time we came to a hill. The admiration, the cheers of his audience, went to his head and encouraged him to fresh extravagances at every mile.

'Aren't they grand?' he said as the children crowded round and bombarded him with their thanks at the end of the day, and secretly we thought so too.

At every stage of the learning process, nursery and number rhymes, jingles and action songs, were of the greatest value, not only because they taught correct intonation, but because they were fun. Some were traditional, others we invented for a particular purpose, and some were old favourites which had to be edited on grounds of religion. 'This little pig' could never, of course, have roast beef, so he had chupattis instead. Then the Muslims objected to the presence of a pig at all. 'Pig is dirty!' shouted an orthodox infant, and actually spat at the offending page. Even pop songs could be turned to good account, and Rolf Harris and the Beatles would have been surprised to know what a help their lyrics could be.

English pronunciation was full of pitfalls for children whose ears were attuned to the subtler, more elusive sounds of Punjabi, and juniors and seniors found it even more difficult than the little ones, whose speech habits were more easily changed. Words beginning with *p* or *f* caused much confusion, since at first the sounds appeared to them to be identical. Those with an ear for language soon recognised the difference, but others continued for weeks to fush and pight, to porget their fencils and lose their fennies. A new recruit to the staff thought she was being addressed in Hindustani when a child asked for 'a fiece of furfle fafer.' For this and other speech difficulties we had a large collection of speech-training rhymes.

Ring games were useful too but old playground favourites, even the simple 'Ring o' Roses,' did not always transplant successfully to Asian soil. An English child plays a ring game with an almost ritual solemnity and decorum. The rules must be obeyed, and whoever is *it* is invested for the moment with an almost magical authority. To the Asian child, the game is as nothing compared with his own part in it. It cannot be enjoyed, in fact it can hardly be tolerated, during the pointless stretches of time when someone else is in the middle. 'In and out the windows' can be chaos and 'Oranges and Lemons' a martyrdom. Even the simple business of forming a circle is a matter for negotiation and argument, and once achieved it is continually breaking up again on grounds of sex and religion, since no Muslim boy, however tiny, will readily suffer the indignity of holding a female hand unless it be that of teacher, for everyone must be next to her.

It was always a red-letter day when a class knew enough English to follow a simple story. In the countryside from which they had so recently come, storytelling was still a living tradition. Squatting in the shade of a mango tree, or crouching round a fire in the fields during the cooler days of winter, they had listened enthralled to the old men of the village as they told heroic legends of their ancestors and stirring tales of their own long-vanished boyhood.

Stories therefore were important, and the traditional English tales, with their repetitive situations and dialogue, were ideal for language teaching. *The Gingerbread Man,* renamed *The Chupatti Man,* was a typical choice with its constantly recurring chorus:

Run, run as fast as you can,
You can't catch me,
I'm the Chupatti man.

After only three or four hearings, the words, 'Run as fast as you can,' began to appear naturally in the context of a game or a race in the playground. Yet story time, which with an English class is a delightful relaxation, was horsework for us in the early stages. However gradual the approach, made through simple talk about colourful pictures, our first attempts at narrative were a trial of patience. With the intense individualism characteristic of their race, the children would hurl themselves separately or collectively upon the illustrations, each shouting out the words he knew. 'That's a tree. Look, a house! It's a street. I can see a car.' Having given their vocabulary an airing, they then transferred their attention to the *next* picture, the events of which had not yet figured in the tale, thereby upsetting its chronology and imparting a *Time and the Conways* effect to the simplest of fiction.

If they had heard the story before, they interrupted continually to tell everyone else what came next and to prove to teacher that they had understood and remembered. If the story was one they disliked or did not wish to hear, they protested at the very first sentence.

'Once upon a time there were three little . . .' I would begin.

'We know! We know!' they shrieked impatiently. 'Once upon a time there were three little pigs. No like.'

''Nother stoory!'

'No, you don't know it!' I said firmly, switching hastily to *Goldilocks*. 'Once upon a time there were three little bears.'

The story had always to be told, not read, and vocabulary reduced to the simplest terms, for if only a few sentences were not understood, the thread was lost and interest evaporated. Once established, however, 'stoory time' was the highlight of the day. It was an enthralling experience to tell the old, loved tales to children who had never heard them before, and to see their fresh, enraptured response. As the crisis drew near, as Little Red Riding Hood was gobbled by the 'vulf', as Jack came belting down the beanstalk with the giant in pursuit, brown eyes grew wide with wonder, chairs edged nearer and nearer, and the front row, in an agony of suspense, gripped my skirt, or taking a pinch of my stocking between finger and thumb, pulled it further and further outward from my leg.

If they were too restless for a story, miming might hold their interest, for the simple games were new and exciting to unsophisticated boys and girls. If individuals were too shy to perform in public, they would act out simple movements together.

We're combing our hair.

We're brushing our teeth.

When they grew braver they acted one at a time, and each was given a picture of a fruit or other item of food, to be kept secret from everyone else. Coming out to the front, he would give me his card, perform his mime, then ask, 'What am I doing?' 'You're eating an apple,' his chosen victim would reply.

Later the game grew more elaborate and the instructions on the card more specific.

Eat a *sour* apple.

Drink some *hot* soup.

Eat some *very good* curry.

The questions, too, became more difficult:

What was he eating?

What was it like?

Did he like it?

What did he do?

At the next stage, the miming of various occupations, the children let themselves go. Policemen bashed demonstrators, teachers flailed away with canes, soldiers lobbed grenades at guerrillas and shopkeepers haggled over mangoes.

The highlight of that first absorbing term was our venture into drama. We decided to produce *The Three Little Pigs*. To do so with a cast of eighteen was an achievement in itself, but somehow I managed it, and by surrounding each piglet with a bevy of relations, contrived to give every member of the class a speaking part. My solitary Muslim, who could not in conscience be a pig, agreed after some heart-searching to be the announcer.

We made paper masks, manufactured our own properties and rehearsed every day until at last we were ready to present a matinée to the school. Gurcharan as the Big Bad Wolf stole the show. 'I am the Big, Bad Vulf!' he roared, advancing menacingly upon the infants who shivered in terror. 'Look out! I am coming down your chimenee. WHOOSH!' We never see him now, a broad-shouldered young man with an engaging elephant-boy smile, without hearing again his wolf-like howl and seeing in imagination his dramatic descent down the chimenee. The applause which greeted our efforts, signifying as it did that we had actually been understood, was heady stuff.

Our second attempt, *Cinderella,* developed unexpected complications, and before it could even be considered by my all-Asian cast it had to be severely censored. The Prince just would not go near Shindoella as they called her, and the courtiers' union, obdurate down to the last and smallest Muslim equerry, backed him up and refused to go within yards of the Ladies in Waiting. Could you possibly have a ballroom scene without a ball? You could—and we did!

Ambition grew with success until the proud day when we presented *Eeyore's Birthday.* The pronunciation of *p* had now been mastered, and Pooh was not Fooh, but it was still touch and go with Winnie. When he strutted in full of confidence his opening announcement, 'I am Vinnie. Vinnie the Po!' was received with applause which surpassed his wildest expectations.

But the star was Gopal, as Piglet, who in the most important scene of the play had to fall on a balloon and burst it. Again and again at rehearsals the balloon fought back. Gopal would lie wriggling and squirming on top of it, contorting his features and panting with his exertions, but in vain. A drawing-pin strategically placed under a chair, but hidden from the spectators, seemed the only solution. He would fall as near to the chair as possible, reach unobtrusively for the pin and prick the balloon.

At the gala performance, however, his groping hand

failed to find the pin. 'Oh, dear, dear! Oh, dear! It's gone!' he cried from his spot on the floor and rolling his eyes at the gallery, which burst into delighted applause. 'Where is the pin? Oh, deary me! Wherever is the pin?' I handed him another. 'Thank you!' he said graciously. 'I'll go back and do it again,' he told his by now enraptured fans, and when a pleasing explosion announced that he had been successful he winked at the house. 'Swinging!' he cried, giving them the thumbs up.

Children we should have liked to keep longer had often to be moved out because, as fresh arrivals streamed in, new classes, new units, were constantly being formed. First the infants would overflow their classroom space, then the juniors would be bursting at the seams. The whole department was for ever growing and dividing like a gigantic amoeba.

'Is there room for one more?' I would ask as I inserted a newcomer into a room already crammed to suffocation.

'You come in,' said Mr Piper, 'pushing the most appealing little thing in front of you, and hiding four hulking brothers and sisters behind your back. I daren't even go to the lavatory, because every time I leave the class you put five more children into it.'

Equipment was always being borrowed and lent and shared, and apparatus whisked from room to room. Even livestock was bandied about.

'Mister Allen wants Ted Poole,' said Aslam standing uncertainly in the doorway.

'He must be in the big school. Go to all the junior classes,' I advised.

Aslam brought his hands together and gave a fair

imitation of the breast-stroke.

'Not Ted Poole boy,' he explained carefully. 'Ted Poole swimming. In jamjar.'

Children who were ready to act in public were almost ready to leave us. Promotions were usually made at the end of every term, and they were never automatic. Only those who were good enough moved up, and competition was therefore keen to be included in the favoured few.

'Please, sir,' said a deputation of six to Mr Piper, 'We will join together to buy you a new shirt if we can go up to Mrs Low's class.'

It was a tempting offer for a young man on the lower rungs of the salary scale, and with a family to support, but I am proud to report that he did not succumb.

Miss Williams, too, was obdurate when two brothers who were determined to stay in her class appeared one Saturday morning at her home with a bunch of plastic daffodils and a see-through nightie.

As our work developed, a number of university lecturers in charge of courses for the teaching of English overseas began to bring their students for school practice. We were almost on their doorstep, and our classes were ideal for their purpose. If at first these young people were disappointed at being sent to us instead of to more glamorous haunts abroad, they soon cheered up, and a few later joined us on the staff.

Our innocent little Punjabis had never heard of such creatures, and there were none of the sly nudges, the knowing winks, the gleeful anticipation of high jinks to come, which herald the arrival of students in more sophisticated quarters. The enthusiastic young men, the charming young women in gay, with-it clothes, were greeted as interesting new acquaintances and perhaps as a welcome change from their sometimes jaded Miss.

Every morning as they leapt from their old cars, their down-at-heel vans and shooting brakes, they carried tote bags and boxes, suitcases and parcels crammed with treasures, strange pieces of apparatus, mobiles, puppet theatres and animated cartoons. Every week there were projects and games, and trips to town, until in the end even the meekest children became intoxicated with their new-found freedom. We were besieged by informers who insisted on telling us just what was happening in the classroom in our absence. 'Come back, Miss!' they would plead. 'Everybody naughty!' One self-appointed monitor, finding verbal denunciation ineffective, brought a daily written list of miscreants from which the only name missing was his own.

Many of our students thought that there was 'a method' of teaching English as a second language, and that it was infallible. We tried to show them that there were as many methods as there were teachers, and that an approach which one teacher found helpful with one class would not necessarily succeed when tried out by another with a different group. We had to impress upon them that we could only show them our respective ways, and that each must work out his own individual style and adapt both methods and material to the type of child he had to teach. For us, knowing the child came first. That, we felt, was the key to successful teaching. Most of the graduates had textbook methods and situations at their fingertips but had not realised that there were no such things as textbook children.

They forgot, too, that our children were learning English as a first language, that the strain upon them was considerable, and that only by alternating oral work with writing or activities could staleness be warded off.

The eager students, pounding away at oral practice or written exercises from nine till four, were reluctant to accept this simple fact. When I went into my classroom to take the register I was greeted with moans and wails and shrieks of indignation. 'Too much work!' the children would cry, and add for my amazement, 'All boards full!' Asghar Ali came up in despair. 'Please tell me,' he pleaded pointing at the mass of hieroglyphics on the blackboard. 'Where am I up to?' For their vigorous new Misses and Sirs the moment of truth tended to dawn at the end of the first week, and when at four o'clock on Friday they tottered wearily into the yard and crawled into their assorted transport, they acknowledged that they, too, were exhausted. 'You must all be tough,' they said as they cranked up and lurched away to recuperate.

By the end of the second week they were beginning to see the wisdom of our ways. 'I have it!' cried one as he came into the staffroom one playtime. 'You act it, crayon it, paint it, cut it out—and stick it!'

A cherished educational theory which had sounded well in the academic calm of the lecture-hall sometimes foundered in the classroom. 'There is no such thing,' another student declared, 'as a child who has no ear for language,' and preceded by a minion carrying margarine, self-raising flour and an egg box, he marched off to give a lesson on groceries. When I went in to see how he was faring I found him pouring salt from a salt-cellar on to his hand, and from there to the floor, repeating most earnestly as he did so, 'It's salt.

It's salt.' The class, delighted with these antics, shouted back with gusto, 'It's sala. It's sala.'

His theory survived until he reached, 'What time is it?' when he came to the conclusion that it was easier for *him* to say, 'What time it is?' than to persevere with the accepted form.

One young man was thrown in at the deep end on his very first morning. He had just settled himself at the back for an hour's observation when Miss was called away. As the door closed behind her, twenty pairs of brown eyes turned speculatively in his direction. Seizing a piece of yellow chalk he drew a circle on the blackboard.

'It's the moon,' he said with an ingratiating smile.

'It's an orange,' chorused the class, which had just learnt about fruit and was sure of its ground.

'It's the moon,' he repeated more firmly. 'In the sky.'

'It's an orange,' repeated the class, also firm.

'No, children! It's the moon. Up there. In the sky.' He pointed to a drift of white cloud moving slowly above the black chimneys.

'It's an orange,' shouted the class, amazed at his stupidity, and annoyed by his refusal to co-operate.

Rubbing it off he drew a careful crescent, as exact a replica as possible of the crescent moon on the Pakistani flag.

'What's this?' he asked, now confident of success.

'It's a banana,' roared the class, almost deafening their Miss who came back just in time to save him.

We felt a little sad when the old cars had lurched away for the last time, for we had grown fond of our students. They had introduced us to the latest methods in language teaching, and had, we hoped, learnt something from us too. They had certainly seen a variety of teaching techniques, and had enjoyed the children, and in the years that followed, a series of exotic post-cards from faraway places, from Nigeria and Pakistan, Uganda and Hong Kong, assured us that we were not forgotten.

So much to learn

Formal language teaching was possible only in short, intensive bouts, and we had to vary the timetable so that interest would be maintained, to intersperse language drills with bursts of lively activity, to ease the mental fatigue of listening to a foreign tongue whilst keeping as closely as possible to the routine of an English school day. Whatever the children were doing, they were being exposed to English, and were unconsciously picking up words connected with the activities in which they were engaged, but until some progress at least had been made in the understanding of English, it was difficult, if not impossible, to introduce most of the normal school subjects.

Children who had been to school before found their new life even harder than those who had received no education at all, for they came with preconceived ideas of what school was like. It was a place where lessons were formal and bookish, where teaching methods were based on learning by rote, on copying and repetition, where discipline was of the strictest, and punishments harsh and frequent. They delighted to show us a curious posture they had been made to adopt before a beating. Bending forward with head well down, and bringing their hands through from behind their knees, they had to grasp the lobes of their ears. This was merely the preliminary to punishment, and they might be left crouching for an hour or more in a position as physi-cally harmful as it was humiliating.

School in England was so different that at first they found it unbelievable, and confronted with our freer methods and friendlier approach some of the older boys did not disguise their scorn. After all their canings and crouchings, our mild reproofs were milk and water. After their incessant learning by rote our attempts to arouse initiative and stimulate self-expression seemed ludicrous. When we urged them to draw and paint and make models, to act small scenes, to dramatise poems and stories and to prance about to music, they looked at us as if we were capering halfwits.

It was wise, we found, to break them in gently, and to begin formally ourselves, otherwise chaos would certainly have followed. Gradually they came to realise that the self-discipline we tried to encourage created a happier atmosphere than oppression, and we for our part began to understand that nervous grins and hysterical giggles were often symptoms of inadequacy and not of ridicule.

Older boys who had reached the higher grades in their Indian or Pakistani schools had already begun to learn English, but an English which was stilted, based on old-fashioned phrases and an out-dated vocabulary, and they had been taught by teachers who, however efficient, had not themselves lost the flat intonation so characteristic of Asia. The English they heard from their Yorkshire teachers was so different, not only in pronunciation but in rhythm and idiom, that for a time it was barely recognisable, and there had to be a period of adjustment to the new sound. Even more confusing were the broad vowels, the strange words and phrases of the local dialect which, in the guise of English, issued from the lips of the boys and girls with whom they played.

These older boys were further dismayed to find themselves for a time at least in a class with children who had never been to school before, who could not even read or write in Urdu or Punjabi. Complete illiterates were in a minority, but some were intelligent boys whose families, by one ruse or another, had evaded authority and kept them at home to work on the land.

Surinder, gentle and slow in thought, speech and movement, had been an elephant boy, a fact which came to light only by chance. Shy because conscious of his inadequacy (it was several weeks before he could trace even the simplest of letters) he sat quietly on the back row watching my antics with a puzzled smile, until the day I held up a picture of an elephant. Before I could even say the word, he darted out to the front, his eyes shining. 'Hathi!' he cried, seizing the book. 'I know hathi! I elephant boy!' With an air of authority impossible to resist, he put his hand on my shoulder and said, 'Down please!' making it plain that I was the elephant, and that he was about to demonstrate his skill on me.

In obedience to his commands I sank to my knees, rose up again, turned left, turned right, and so vivid were his gestures, so compelling his desire to communicate, that I instinctively obeyed and realised only afterwards that all his commands had been given in Punjabi. The class watched spellbound and when suddenly he stopped, overcome with embarrassment at finding himself the centre of attention, they applauded wildly. 'Lovely elephant boy!' they said patting him enthusiastically on the shoulder, then not wanting me to feel left out they turned to me. 'And you,' they added, 'are a very lovely elephant.'

These older boys who came to us completely illiterate, and with perhaps only a year of school ahead of them, were dismayed at having to learn basic infant skills when all they really wanted to do was to go out to work, and Surinder was no exception, but he struggled on and could read and write a little before he left us.

The children most disillusioned about English education were undoubtedly the very youngest, whose aspiring parents had painstakingly taught them the alphabet from A to Z. As I led the offspring to its allotted class, it would tug at my skirt, chirping out endless A B C D E F Gs. 'He know A B C,' said the father proudly, convinced that this information, so laboriously acquired, would open the door to a higher education.

They had so many new skills to master, so many adjustments to make in their approach to learning, that it was never difficult to make profitable use of the time between language sessions. In every age group there were boys and girls who had never been to school before and who lacked the basic skills taken for granted in a western infants' school.

Until we watched them struggling to use scissors, to

colour with crayons, to paint or even to use a pencil, we had never realised just how much an English infant learns in its pre-school years from sense-training, constructional and educational toys, from scribbling and drawing, from books and pictures, and above all from a mother who reads stories, talks to and plays with the child from its earliest days.

At home in the Punjab our boys and girls had never handled play material specifically designed to develop manual control or dexterity. Not only were their fingers poker stiff, but they were utterly at a loss when first presented with sense-training toys and play material. They had no idea how to use them or what to do with them, and showed no initiative whatever. With amazement we saw them standing passive in front of sand and water trays and even beside the dressing-up box, waiting to be told what they were expected to do.

In spite of our help and encouragement, their apprenticeship to play was a long one, and with the little ones the first phase was often destructive. Whilst decorous English infants patted sand pies and castles, made paper boats and sailed them, in Class 1 sand flew through the air, water play raged in illegitimate places, the Wendy House was awash, and action painting of the most genuine kind flourished around the easels.

Most parents failed to realise that in the changed circumstances of their lives the children desperately needed toys with which to occupy themselves during long winter evenings and weekends. Many whose homes we visited had less to entertain them than even the most poverty-stricken English child, no books, no toys, no comics, not even a scrap of paper or a pencil, and if father was on night work they had to keep quiet because he was sleeping upstairs. It was not surprising that the little ones came whooping to school each morning bouncing and boisterous, and hurled themselves frantically upon the toys, or that they were always more of a handful than usual on Mondays.

These difficulties will certainly pass. There are now welcome signs that the children themselves are clamouring for books and toys, and we have watched Asian mothers yielding to pressure in Woolworths and elsewhere, and seen children buying crayons and exercise books on their own account. In some families too, there has been an encouraging carry-over from the older boys and girls who were our earliest pupils, and who are making sure that their young brothers and sisters have the playthings of which they themselves had been deprived.

In almost every home, however, there was a television set. Covered with a beautiful plush cloth when not in use, it was of course a status symbol, but the children found it absorbing and learnt a great deal of English while viewing. Advertising slogans, jingles and other catch phrases were picked up and imitated without effort, popping out in the most unexpected contexts.

'Where's your book?' I asked Abbas, who was only five.

'It's on top of the pops,' he replied, pointing to the top of the cupboard.

Dr Who and Tarzan, the Wild West and Tom and Jerry, were soon as familiar to our Jaswinders and Abduls as to every white boy, and popular programmes gave English and Asian a common topic of conversation and a store of shared experience.

There were juniors and even seniors who did not know how to hold a pencil. Teenage boys would grasp it in the fist as if it were a hand scythe, or stab at the paper, or even wait to be shown which end to use. Those who had already received some education had to learn to write all over again and found themselves frustrated and confused, for Punjabi script, though flowing like English from left to right, has entirely different symbols and on a ruled page hangs like washing *below* the line. As for Urdu, its beautiful, decorative Arabic characters proceed from right to left, and those who had acquired it had to be retrained to drag the pencil over the page instead of pushing it. For seniors as well as juniors, writing practice was therefore a daily necessity. Even when western script had been mastered, and the Urdu-speaking children had learnt to begin on the left-hand side of the page, they would still from force of habit write individual words backwards, including their names and 'yadseuT si yadoT' was so common an opening to the daily news that it began to look normal to us as well. But as with small children whose first script is mirror writing, this difficulty eventually resolved itself, and continual correction merely increased the child's anxiety.

The concept of left and right is one which many intelligent children find difficult to grasp, and to these Pakistani youngsters who already had so many other adaptations to make it could be a formidable obstacle. A real effort of will was needed to remember to open a book at the front and not at the back, or to begin using a new exercise book on the first page instead of last. A coloured star stuck on every top left-hand corner helped to clear up the confusion and showed the child where to begin writing. The transition from right to left was hardest of all for the well-educated, compelled as they were to relearn their basic techniques, and they must have felt all the baffled irritation, all the discouragement and frustration, of a born left-hander forced by circumstances to rely wholly on his right.

The older Indians and Pakistanis enjoyed number work and revelled in mechanical arithmetic, in which they had been thoroughly grounded in their village schools, where multiplication tables were child's play, and far from ending officially at twelve times, continued well on into the twenties. Sums were therefore a welcome relaxation from oral work, but here again the barrier of language intervened, for before working from an English textbook they had to acquire a number vocabulary, to learn the words add, subtract, multiply and divide, as well as the nouns associated with them, whilst problems were out of the question until a fairly high standard of English had been reached.

Of all the subjects with which we sought to extend a knowledge of English, craft and handwork proved the most rewarding. They not only set tongues wagging, for the children loved to chatter both to me and to each other as they snipped and hammered and glued, but they required a rich vocabulary, the names of tools and materials, of shapes and colours, measurements, sizes, processes and a wealth of common verbs, all of which were being unconsciously assimilated as they worked. Most important of all, these activities linked up perfectly with the vocabulary and structures already learnt. Models of houses, of furniture, boats, cars, the street, the town, all served to reinforce the language lessons which had preceded them.

The most ambitious project of all was Mr Piper's island. Mr Piper was gifted, young and enthusiastic. He was also original, and the island was to be his masterpiece. Made of *papier mâché* and rising high in a corner of the room, it was to contain a town, in fact a civilisation of its own, and to be the centre of his language teaching, the *point de départ* of innumerable topics.

That at least was the idea, but he had not realised how long it would take children to mix and make a mound of the size he wanted. For weeks the stairs were crowded with Indians staggering up and down with buckets, and Pakistanis stiffening slowly as the paste dried on their persons. The room rang with shrieks and cries as all nationalities pounded away, merrily mashing up the *Guardian* and *The Times* whilst the tall, imperturbable young man stood in the middle viewing his creation and finding it good. The caretaker was less impressed.

There was one other fact of life which had escaped Mr Piper. He did not know that *papier mâché,* like man, both ages and decays. During the half-term break, nature took a hand, and when we returned, the island was covered with mould and a thick grey fungus smothered the streets of its capital. Even Mr Piper, who loved it, had to admit that it smelled—and he had not even begun the first of his projects. It finished up in the dustbin, or rather in a series of dustbins.

'By gum! This lot's 'eavy!' said the dustman. 'They must ha' put t' Taj Mahal in 'ere!'

Mr Piper's second island was more ambitious. It was 4ft square and was concreted to the floor on a base of rubble collected by the children from one of the demolition sites in which the area abounded. There was even a moat round it with a neat little plug for drainage. The island itself, rising from its stone platform, was a mound of earth from the school garden. The caretaker, alternating between rage and black despair, stumped in and out and dropped hints about his union. We saw his point. The mess was indescribable, but the room was always alive and active, and the amount of English the children acquired, though never consciously learnt, was incalculable.

The island was sown with seeds, and miniature forests covered the hillsides. The moat was busy with craft of every kind. Roads were built around and across it. A village sprang up, then a town connected to it by a railway network, but in the end this island too had to go, for Mr Piper had been called to foreign parts and no one else felt equal to creating mountains and engineering moats, or to facing the caretaker.

The parting was sad, but its demolition was as dramatic as its construction. Through the open window ran a simple pulley made of rope and a bucket. The children, chain-gang fashion, hacked the island to pieces, loaded them into buckets, and lowered them to the ground, where yet another chain-gang received the mess and carried it back to the building site.

'Dust to dust . . .' said Mr Piper mournfully as his creation crumbled before his eyes, but born teacher that he was, he cheered up when it occurred to him how good all this would be not only for their English, but for their experience. He became almost jaunty as rocks hurtled round him and the last remnants of the moat gurgled down the Art Room sink.

Art was a disappointment. Remembering the beauty of Indian rugs and brassware, the intricacy of Indian sculpture, the exquisite frescoes of the caves of Ajanta, I had expected to be dazzled by oriental pattern and design. Not only was there no dazzle, there was no design. Always, no matter how bright the class, I was presented with an exact replica of whatever I was sketching on the blackboard and always, when it came to colour, the children seemed incapable of deciding for themselves. 'Blue?' they would enquire hopefully. 'Green? Shall I use yellow?' When I asked them to draw a picture they stared at me, their big brown eyes wide with amazement, or simply put down their pencils and said flatly, 'Can't! You do it!'

With the older boys in particular an art lesson could develop into a battle of wills, for some made no attempt to hide their scorn. This, they intimated, was girls' stuff, useless rubbish, a waste of time, and it had nothing to do with education. They put brush to paper with the patronising air of one humouring a halfwit. The more co-operative did what they could, but as a concession to me rather than from any conviction that the exercise was of value.

Other teachers of Muslim children sometimes told me that their pupils were reluctant to draw men or women, since Islamic law forbade any representation of the human form, but the taboo was never in evidence in any of my classes, perhaps because for me they would never draw anything at all except an occasional arrangement of formalised flowers.

There was, however, one creative activity into which the children entered with zest, and which proved to be a genuine means of self-expression. That was modelling.

Few had seen plasticine before and there were infants

who tried to eat it, but once they had been shown how to roll and model it there were instant cries of recognition. 'Mytti!' they exclaimed in delight, and set to work with a will. 'Mytti' was earth or clay, which in their sun-baked villages they had shaped and fashioned into playthings. This was a medium they could handle without difficulty. The direct contact with a primitive material brought a surge of creative joy, and as they pounded and squeezed, imagination stirred and a host of submerged memories flooded back into consciousness.

The objects they made with such obvious pleasure belonged always and wholly to their own village culture. They invariably began by modelling a fat, square cow with enormous horns, a pronounced hump, and no legs, a curious omission which I explained away both to myself and the children by saying, 'She's sitting down.'

Next in popularity came grinding stones exactly like the Stone Age querns turned up on archaeological sites. Little girls in particular made them with loving care and showed us how they were used, for corn is still ground by hand in the Indian countryside and the work is done by women.

Most of the models were of homely objects, cooking pots straight from the *Arabian Nights,* with unmistakably oriental lids, baskets of eggs, piles of chupattis. Becoming more ambitious, the girls turned next to jewellery and walked proudly up and down adorned with plasticine rings and bangles.

Geography, history, nature study and science, could not be taught as such, for though some children had adequate background knowledge they had no English, and many had neither. They had no framework of fact within which a Junior School curriculum would have made sense. Our teaching of General Interest Studies, as we preferred to call them, had therefore to be adaptable and fluid. The aim was to give meaning to a perplexing new environment. The method was to start from what was known, from topics dealt with in class, from everyday scenes and activities, from local and national events, and to build upon those, taking care that the language used was well within their understanding.

Everyday happenings were a valuable starting point. We discussed the weather in all its aspects and pointed out its importance as a conversational gambit in any casual English encounter. From there we moved on to the seasons and the changes they brought in nature and in our way of life, stressing the need to adapt clothing accordingly.

The annual festivals, Christmas, Easter, Whitsuntide and Harvest were explained and celebrated. So too were Pancake Tuesday, 'Chupatti Day,' Hallowe'en and Bonfire Night. 'We're havin' a bunfire!' they told us gleefully. (The local idiom was beginning to make its mark.) We attended exhibitions, the fair and entertainments in the park.

Nature study meant learning about English animals and birds, about plants and flowers. One aspect of the subject, the ordering and planting of bulbs, taxed our ingenuity to the utmost. Waving catalogues and plastic daffodils (we had been buying the same detergent for weeks) we strove to explain how the flower would emerge from the bulb, or as they persisted in calling it, 'the onion.' 'Look!' they exclaimed as we poured fibre from the bag. 'Chicken toilet!'

The introductory talk was followed by what Latif

called the orderation. 'Ask Daddy how many you can buy,' we said as we dealt out the order forms. 'Tell him to write the number on the paper and *bring it back.*'

The message had been received but not understood. The few forms which had not been blown away in transit, or fashioned into darts, or swallowed by the baby, trickled back over the next few days numberless, nameless, bearing the single word *Yes,* or *All.* Azaf ordered one snowdrop and 3lb of fibre.

By the time the Bulb Show came round, many children had moved on to other schools bearing their onions with them, but the exhibits of those who remained added immensely to the originality of the display. The judge stood transfixed before Ghulam's flowering carrot-tops, Shafik's sprouting horse-chestnut and Pergee's illegitimate castor-oil plant. Crocuses peered out of cocoa tins, hyacinths did their stunted best in bean cans, daffodils nodded from mugs and beakers, and Zarina's scarlet tulips blazed from a rose-decked chamberpot. Her delighted smile as she received the consolation prize was ample compensation for all our efforts.

Geography was the one subject in which it was possible to follow the normal school syllabus. We made plans of the school, the town and the heavy woollen districts. Each child marked his father's place of work, an exercise which gave us interesting information about the types of employment in which Asian immigrants were engaged. Jobs in public transport and night work in mills and foundries predominated. We traced maps of the Punjab and found the places where fathers used to work, slipping in a little language practice, for a topic like this lent itself to changes of tense.

My father works in a mill in England.
He worked on a farm in the Punjab.

We discovered that some children were quite familiar with weaving terms. A boy who appeared to have no word of English suddenly said, 'Dobcross Loom!' when he saw one in a picture. He had actually used one in India. At the museum it was the textile section which aroused most enthusiasm, and a nineteenth-century handloom was greeted like an old friend. 'My grandmother, she's got one like this!' they cried, and could hardly be persuaded to leave so nostalgic a link with home.

They learnt to trace their journeys from India and Pakistan, excitedly following their individual routes with toy boats, trains and aeroplanes, and the story of their travels was always interesting. One family had come overland through Persia in a rickety old van which had been brought to a halt every few miles when a wheel fell off. Another had arrived in London with instructions to take a taxi to King's Cross where they could board a train for the north. The length of the taxi ride amazed them. London must indeed be enormous, they reflected, as minutes gave way to hours, and their innocent surprise continued until they were deposited on the doorstep of their relatives, who were thrilled to see them but were less enthusiastic about the bill. The driver, perhaps by accident but more probably by design, had 'misunderstood,' and this was not by any means an isolated case.

If geography was a natural winner, history had everything against it, since lack of western background, lack of time sense, the linguistic difficulties of the past tense with its maddening irregularities, all made it a problem subject.

It seemed wisest to take a topic in which they already had an interest and to follow it backward in time. We discussed, observed and drew cars, railway engines, ships, aeroplanes and clothes of the present day, then traced their evolution down the years.

When I was a little girl, clothes were like this.
When my mother was a little girl . . .
When my grandmother was a little girl . . .

It seemed to work until Shaista produced a drawing of Neanderthal man, club in hand, sitting on a sofa at the entrance to his cave and wearing a Marks & Spencer pullover.

History through the lives of the great was always popular, for the children had an insatiable appetite for stories, and their comments on the famous were refreshing. Christopher Columbus, though impossible to pronounce, was 'a very good boatman.' King Alfred and the chupattis made them laugh. 'A very silly rajah!' said Rashida, and took the tale home to father, who told it to his friends in the 'fectory', where apparently it brought the house down. Florence Nightingale, who shared their passion for hospitals, was taken at once to their hearts. They shook their fists at her critics, 'very bad men,' cheered the Light Brigade to the echo, and trussed each other up in bandages. 'Tell us again,' they begged next day, 'all about Florence Nightingown.'

Though Clio emerged a little battered from these encounters, the fascination of great events, the magic of powerful personalities, remained in the children's minds, and they were learning the basic stories which form part of the heritage of every English boy or girl.

The hospital—doctor topic was typical of many which had a social as well as a linguistic content, for hospitals were a feature of their lives and a commonplace of their conversation. Their mothers, for obvious reasons, were constantly in and out, and when in a book on the subject we reached a picture of the maternity ward, there was a ripple of excitement. 'All those ladies,' said Ghulam, 'have got big tummies.' The class nodded and clucked in complete understanding.

From hospitals and doctors we moved on to anatomy. A small model of a skeleton was received with awe. Some stared in silence, others fingered their own bones. Only Abbas found adequate words.

'But who,' he said slowly, 'has eaten the meat?' It was a difficult one to answer.

'Nobody's eaten it,' I said. 'It fell off when he'd been dead a long time.' It was the best I could manage on the spur of the moment, since their vocabulary could not encompass mortality and decay.

Astounded and at first incredulous, they learnt that they had hearts which beat and blood which swished about inside them. One class taught by a doctor's daughter even had a stethoscope. The boys ripped open their shirts and clamoured for a turn, whilst the girls had to be content with such muffled thumps as could be heard through a kameez and layers of vest.

When the seniors were absorbed in a study of the bloodstream, an Indian parent arriving with a message for his son was more puzzled than ever about English education when he saw the children peering at themselves and at each other in the search for 'weins,' not always easy to trace under brown skin. Hamid, who was darker than the rest, had given it up, and tired of looking for what did not appear to be there, had stationed himself in the passage to wait for a white man, under whose pale outer casing they might more readily be discerned.

We came to realise that scenes like these, glimpsed out of context and wholly misunderstood, could cause genuine distress, even anger, to fathers who had brought sons to England for the sole purpose of giving them an English education. 'Weins' in Asia were in textbooks, not in human beings, and the modern approach to learning through observation, discovery, experiment, reality, was mistaken for slackness and lack of discipline. Some even sent their boys back to India or Pakistan because, as they told us not without a hint of malice, they had found places for them in 'good' schools.

Anatomy was followed by hygiene. We talked about clean hair, hoping, though in vain, to get rid of hair oil, and about dental care, for the white teeth which made their smiles so attractive were soon ruined by bubble gum and lollipops. I took my class to the launderette, and also tackled the subject of food hygiene, hoping that some of the hints would find their way home to mother.

Since many of our girls were quite mature we gave them a few simple lessons about the onset of puberty, but it was a difficult decision to take, since sex education is as taboo in Asian families as ever it was in Victorian England.

The last half-hour of the day had to be given over to relaxation, for by three o'clock the strain of listening to a foreign language was beginning to tell on even the brightest child. The older ones just switched themselves off and infants often fell asleep.

It was not easy to find activities which did not involve English in some form or another. There were films. 'Walky walky ones!' they cried when from film strips we graduated to a ciné projector. There were jigsaws and ludo, halma and snakes and ladders, and how reminiscently they shuddered as they whipped their tiddlywinks down the scaly backs! Since all these diversions were new and strange they had to be taught how to play every game and even shown what to do with a jigsaw.

With the beginners this last period was conducted wholly in Punjabi. To the younger ones Asian staff told stories about or from India and Pakistan, and with the seniors they discussed topical events in their respective countries, by all of which a link was maintained with their own folk-lore, history and culture.

Physical education brought trials all its own, for our brocaded ladies were inclined to be lazy. By cajolery and guile, melting away in the direction of the lavatories, writhing in feigned agony, pointing dolefully to a scratch or a pimple, they did all they could to put off the lesson. 'No PE!' they would wail. 'Very poorly!' 'Legs not going!' Drooping over their desks in a most convincing display of languor, they would trot out their favourite ploy. 'My head is paining me!' they would say. Then when we showed no sign of softening, 'Belly very hurting!' This they clearly thought would be a winner.

The real cause of their aversion lay deeper. They claimed that their religion made it a sin to bare their legs, and compelled them to wear the shalwar at all times. Stubbornly, unanimously, they refused to change, declaring that knickers and vest revealed too much of the human form to be worn in the presence of males.

When I took the girls to be kitted out, some would not even hold the accursed garments, and I had to stuff them unceremoniously beneath their arms or into the waistband of their shalwar. 'Nahin! Nahin!' they wailed, and I blenched as I thought of the next battle to be waged, that of actually getting them inside the offending pants.

Letters angry, peremptory, pleading, threatening began to pour in. 'Respectfully I beg to say,' wrote one parent, 'that we cannot let Shafira play with Jym wearing underwear. Please may I request to let them play wearing trousers.' Another threw the outfit provided on the fire.

A compromise had to be reached. The Muslim teachers working for the Authority tried to explain to rebel families that the strict code of conduct for Muslim women did not apply until girls were of marriageable age, but they were not successful. Being only teachers, and not the religious leaders of the community, they could not force their views upon devout families.

We began the stripping gradually and proceeded by easy stages. At first they changed into knickers but were allowed to keep their petticoats on, and the resulting silhouettes had to be seen to be believed. Enormous bloomers topped the thinnest of legs, for they had tucked in, not one petticoat, but three. Later the petticoats too came off and the class looked almost normal. Almost, but not quite! In their attempts to hide the offending limbs, the gymnasts had pulled their knicker legs as far down as nature and elastic would allow, in almost every case below the knee, and the crotch, in consequence, came somewhere in the region of the calf, with grotesque results whenever they tried to run or jump.

Yet this phase too finally passed, and when the girls left us they were seasoned changers. Those of us who had watched the transformation could not help but admire the way in which they overcame their intense shyness, and the courage with which they conquered a belief, inherited by generations of Muslim women, that all parts of the body must be covered in case the one inch exposed 'should burn in hell for ever.'

With such a fate continually held before them, senior girls understandably refused to change for swimming, and families began to keep their daughters away from school on swimming days. Even when the authorities provided one girl with a leotard her father remained adamant. He held that the garment, though ostensibly covering the child's body, was just as revealing as any swimming costume, and his personal interpretation of the Koran was that no female should disclose her limbs in the presence of males.

It was one of the cases in which the absence of a professional priesthood in Islam was a disadvantage, for it meant that there was no one person in the Muslim community who could give an authoritative ruling.

The unco-operative father was obeying the dictates of his own conscience. The child herself, caught between two factions, would have liked nothing better than to conform.

In spite of such difficulties the weekly session at the baths was always enjoyable. The crocodile of thirty Asians walking through the town on a busy Friday afternoon naturally attracted attention. We had to run the gauntlet of catcalls, wolf whistles, quips and stares both curious and hostile. One middle-aged shopper would stop as we passed and mutter, 'Disgusting! Disgusting!' I never had time to ask her why, being far too busy shepherding my flock.

We had an interested and well-disposed public too, especially when we had to hold up the traffic in order to cross the main road. First the neat line of seniors would cross in order, then the straggling juniors, and finally, long, long after everyone else, tiny Baksheesh, wearing a huge black waterproof cap of his father's, would extricate himself from the legs of the crowd to come dashing wildly across the zebra. He always delighted our regular audience of workmen, who actually missed him if he was absent.

'Weer's 'im wi't cap, love?' they would ask grinning. 'Has 'e fallen ovver it?'

Sometimes too, as I stood on that crossing watching the crocodile file past, I thought it would never come to an end. It had, in fact, increased enormously in length, having been more than doubled by the addition of friends and relatives who had tagged on at the back as it passed their homes.

Once inside, the fun really began. Most English children are a little apprehensive on their first visit to the baths. Not so our Asians! The problem was not to coax them into the water, but to stop them from drowning in it, and only by force could we restrain them from jumping in at the deep end before the lesson had even begun.

Juniors were less reluctant than seniors to buy swimming trunks and costumes, although little local difficulties arose when they tried to put them on. Kalsoom came down from the changing rooms in a beautiful swimsuit of turquoise satin. The bodice was ruched and tucked and cut away to fit the bust. It was charming, and the effect was enhanced by the fact that all this ruching was at Kalsoom's back! She watched carefully as I explained, with demonstrations, that fronts were fronts, especially when ruched, and that backs could never take their place. I felt a glow of pride when the next week she came down the steps looking neat and trim. Only after the lesson was it apparent that something had gone wrong. As she climbed out of the bath a long green tail flapped wetly behind her. It was the knicker section of her swimsuit. She had put her legs not through the holes, but through the mock skirt. To all intents and purposes she had not had the suit on at all.

Then there was Prem. Poor Prem! His trunks were too big, and every time he had a session at the practice bar he was in difficulties. If he held on to the bar his trunks floated off. If he held on to his trunks, he sank.

Ootar sank whatever she did. Right to the bottom she would go, face downwards, her body as flat as a pancake. 'Come up, Ootar! Come up!' the instructress and I would implore from the edge of the bath, and slowly, without the least change of position, Ootar's bottom would emerge and then Ootar's grin. When she did master the art, she swam like a hinge, opening and shutting all the time. But she swam!

What a line-up those first swimmers were! The boys, handsome and bronzed in their bright coloured trunks, the girls so thin in their beautiful swimsuits, some still adorned with price-tags. Once I had an unwitting glimpse of how they looked to the general public. As one of the boys in his mock leopard-skin trunks ran down the stairs to wash his feet, a swimmer just finishing his cup of tea in the café nudged his companion.

'Look!' he said. 'Sabu!'

Objections to changing were trivial compared to the difficulties which arose with dancing, for here a serious moral issue was involved. In Punjabi villages dancing in public was an activity denied to all but prostitutes or fallen women, yet it was a part of the normal English school curriculum, and somehow prejudice would have to be overcome. A change of name to Music and Movement deceived no one, for even if you were pretending to be a leaf in the wind you were twirling and swaying, and what was that but dancing?

The visiting teacher was at first bewildered when time after time her class of teenage girls rushed shrieking in panic to the cloakroom. A *man* had entered the hall!

Once it was an unsuspecting joiner. Hammer in hand, he stood rooted to the spot as screaming girls shot past him. She made frantic signals for him to leave.

'Nay, love!' he said mildly. 'Don't bother about me. I've seen t' dance o't seven veils.' He was, after all, a man of the world.

'It's not you!' she wailed. 'It's these girls. If their

parents know you've seen them like this, they'll be dishonoured for life.'

'Dishonoured be blowed!' replied the man of the world a little testily. 'What about me if them window-frames isn't finished by dinner-time?'

In the end a compromise was reached. If he promised not to look he could go through, so covering his eyes with his hand and remarking that foreigners were queer, he stumbled uncertainly to his work, feeling his way along the wall bars.

Dancing in pairs was another tricky procedure. Muslim boys would hold hands with Muslim boys and Sikh with Sikh, but only under duress would Muslim partner Sikh, whilst dancing with girls was impossible. The aversion has never been completely overcome, and resistance still breaks out periodically in schools to which the seniors have been dispersed.

The early games lessons were a shambles. Not wishing to force the issue we at first allowed the girls to play netball in full regalia. The referee's whistle was never silent. 'All right!' she would say. 'Where is it now?' and the game came to a standstill whilst hapless Muslims struggled to extricate the ball from their silks and satins.

The boys were not at first enthusiastic about football. 'Too much kicky!' they complained, but encouraged and coached by the men on the staff they accepted and then enjoyed it.

There was, however, one aspect of the sporting life for which no one had thought to prepare them. Invited to play a friendly game of soccer with a neighbouring school, they went, they changed, they played happily enough, but after the match they were sent into the showers. They were almost rigid with shock. Tall, handsome Sharif, marched out with dignity, attaché case in hand, and vowed he would never go in again. Prem came running out in sheer fright. Manzoor clapped his hands over his eyes as if to erase the memory of the scene for ever, and poor little Mangi felt sick.

'It's quite all right. Just try it! You'll like it,' urged the master in charge, but his voice was lost in the cries of decency outraged. Each boy in his own way was adamant. On that occasion they won, but later, as with everything else that was new and strange, even the showers came to be accepted.

When the cricket season came round we allowed ourselves to hope for better things. Here, we told each other, was a game which both Indians and Pakistanis played with grace and skill. With a wealth of natural talent at our disposal, we were on to a good thing. Effortlessly as a six by Freddy Trueman our Anglo-Asian team would rise to the top of the Junior Schools League and stay there. Yet somehow it never seemed to work out that way. Week after week they returned defeated by teams from schools in prosperous suburbs.

'It wasn't that I minded losing,' said the Deputy Head as he led his dejected eleven back to the cloakroom, 'but there was the opposing team all dolled up in spotless whites, and there were our poor little beggars, the opening batsman in faded jeans, a pullover full of holes, and that old fur hat he insists on wearing all the time. Number Two had torn pants. Number Three was a Pakistani in what looked like pyjama bottoms, and Number Four was an Indian in a navy blue suit complete with waistcoat and tie—and even

139

gloves! I couldn't bear to look at the rest.'

'Never mind!' said a colleague consolingly. 'I'll make you a set of white armbands for the next match.'

Practice there was in plenty, but it never seemed to make perfect.

'How are they shaping?' I asked an Indian colleague as he led our budding Ranjis back from a coaching session in the park.

'Not good at all,' he said in a gloomy tone. 'They do not play according to the rules, since each one craves a turn.'

'Each one craves a turn.' It could have been the national motto.

Feasts and festivals

Since ours was a school of many races it was also a school of many faiths. Among the children who at dinner-time, eyes closed, hands together, so decorously thanked God for what they were about to receive, there were adherents of five of the world's great religions, Muslims, Hindus, Sikhs, an occasional Buddhist and a wide variety of Christians.

The authors of the 1944 Education Act probably never envisaged such a mixed community assembled for worship in an English primary school. They stated that religious instruction must be given daily in every county and voluntary school, a requirement we found it impossible to fulfil. Lack of English alone was an insuperable obstacle, and even when they had acquired a fair grasp of the language the children were with us for so short a time that systematic instruction was hardly possible.

All we could do was to explain the Christian faith in so far as it affected their lives in England, and to tell them those stories from the New Testament which would enable them to understand the great festivals of Christmas, Easter and Whitsuntide. We discussed the Hindu, Sikh and Muslim faiths, too, whenever their feasts or fasts came round, and never missed an opportunity of pointing out how many religions there were in the world. The occasional presence in our classes of a European Catholic or a Chinese Buddhist brought home more clearly than words the truths we were trying to convey.

Once our children had moved into the main school they shared the scripture lessons of their English class. Their parents could have asked for them to be withdrawn from religious instruction, but very few did so.

Boys and girls of both communities were, of course, taught the basic truths of their faith in schools at temple and mosque. Little Muslims learnt to recite the Koran, and bright Sikh boys were trained to read the *Granth Sahib,* which enshrines the teaching of their ten great gurus, so that they could take their turn in intoning it aloud during services in the temple. Its script was archaic and difficult, and had to be mastered before the reader was allowed to take part in public worship.

These schools were not exclusively religious. Children were taught to read and write in Urdu and Punjabi, and every attempt was made to maintain the link with their own history and culture, and to foster their national identity. 'Miss!' they would call if we met them plodding home with satchels full of books. 'We've been to Indian school,' and proudly they showed us their exercises for the week, written in script so subtle and elaborate that we could only marvel at the tenacity which had enabled them to learn it.

Morning assembly, an aspect of religion which might have been expected to arouse controversy, never became an issue at all, a fact we found surprising. The beginners did not attend, since they would have gained nothing from a service which was totally incomprehensible, but children who had made some progress in understanding took part on special occasions, whilst the most advanced joined the main school every Friday.

Only one attempt was made to interfere with morning prayers, and that was not a request for withdrawal, but a demand that certain hymns be omitted when Muslim boys and girls were present. The Imam had obtained a copy of the school hymnbook and listed a number of hymns he regarded as too heretical to be acceptable. That he should apparently acquiesce in the rest of our worship was so unexpected as to be almost incredible.

The children themselves enjoyed the experience, for attendance at prayers marked the end of their apprenticeship in English. Now at last they were an integral part of the school. Linguistically speaking they had arrived. At first they prayed quietly to themselves but soon began to join in naturally with the rest. Though unaccustomed to western music, they tried valiantly to sing, and visitors who had not been forewarned thought their ears were out of order when, beneath the familiar notes of 'All things bright and beautiful', they detected a rumbling ground bass, toneless, tuneless and timeless, a kind of descant in reverse. It gave the hymn what the world of pop would call a backing, but odd though it was, we liked to hear it, and encouraged the children to continue, for it meant that they were contributing as fully as they could to the communal experience.

Difficulties arising from religion did not always spring from the differences between East and West, but from those between East and East. When the Sikhs were in a majority there were no disturbances, but with the gradual increase of Pakistanis the situation was reversed and Muslims soon outnumbered Sikhs by two to one. Then rivalry became more pronounced. One group of Muslims refused to take their milk if it had been given out by a Sikh, an issue which had to be resolved with all the diplomacy I could muster, but I, too, had my obstinate moments and refused to sacrifice my classroom routine or personal ideals to rebellions such as these.

Although Muslim and Sikh learnt to work and play together and seemed friendly enough, enmity lay just below the surface. It needed only a slight argument to bring it out into the open, and whenever political trouble between India and Pakistan flared up afresh, the repercussions in school were instantaneous and sometimes unpleasant. During the Kashmir dispute feelings ran high, but a determined and open show of friendship and mutual courtesy by our Sikh and Muslim colleagues helped considerably to lower the temperature.

The death of Mr Nehru was greeted with open jubilation by the more militant Muslims. 'Pundit Nehru no good. Very glad him dead!' they said, making sure that the distressed and weeping Indians could hear them.

The most innocent situations could provoke an outburst of rivalry.

'What are you making?' an interested group asked

144

Infants' Miss as she shaped a feather head-dress for the occupants of the wigwam.

'A Red Indian Hat,' she said, holding it up for inspection.

'Not a Red Indian hat!' Javed protested angrily. 'Red Pakistani hat!'

And so it had to be. The voice of nationalism had spoken.

Jamila, a fervent little Muslim, did her best to push me off the fence on which I so determinedly sat. In a series of drawings purporting to illustrate my activities, my left hand was shown in a variety of occupations, but my right, in every picture, was brandishing a Pakistani flag.

Most differences, however, were settled amicably. I once tried to show them that though we were Christian, Sikh, Hindu and Muslim, and worshipped in different ways, we should and could live in peace together. Hoping to extend their horizons still further I produced a picture of the Buddha and Buddhist monks. This was too much for Akhtar. For him, fervent Muslim that he was, I had reached the limit. 'What!' he shouted. 'Another God! How many Gods have you then?' The picture was not allowed to remain on the wall.

It is of the very nature of Islam to proselytise and vigorously to spread the faith, and there were times when this zeal for converts stirred even the tolerant Sikhs to protest.

Allah Ditta, an intelligent and handsome boy of nine, was always eager to tell the class a story in Punjabi whilst teacher coped with the attendance percentages or wrestled with the dinner books.

Once during his oration I sensed rather than saw that something was amiss, and looked up to find him in full throttle. His face had turned a dull red and his eyes flashed as a torrent of impassioned words poured from his lips. He seemed oblivious of me and even of his audience, which looked shaken and unhappy. I was alarmed.

'Ditta! Ditta!' I said sharply. 'What are you telling them?' My voice seemed to awaken him to reality.

'I was only telling them,' he said, 'about the Holy Prophet who was burnt to death because he was a Muslim, but God told him that the flames were only roses and so he felt no burning.'

'Miss! Miss!' shouted a Sikh dissenter. 'He was also saying that we must all be Muslims. All the world must be Muslims. We don't like!'

He was never allowed to tell a story again.

At rare intervals we admitted an Indian Christian. The father of one of them insisted that his boy should be moved into an English class as soon as possible. 'I don't want him mixing with them Hindus and Muslims,' he said. 'We're Christians.'

Islam, like Christianity, has a variety of sects, and one of the most evangelistic of these had some hundred adherents in the town, living together in a closely knit community and worshipping in their own small mosque. Since women were not permitted to attend their religious services, Infants' Miss and I were surprised, as well as honoured, to receive an invitation to meet their world leader who, on a tour of European mosques, was paying a brief visit to the town.

Anxious not to be late (*At eleven sharp,* said the invitation) and with heads and arms discreetly covered, we hurried past open mill windows through which the clatter of looms floated out on to the summer air, to the small back street in which every house was occupied by a member of the sect, and by families who were closely inter-related.

The mosque, a converted terrace house, was newly white-washed and gay with flags and garlands of flowers. Outside in the sunshine groups of Pakistanis and reporters stood waiting, and small Muslim boys, like sheepdogs rounding up intransigent ewes, chased stray Muslim girls up the path of the adjacent house and shut them firmly in, for great though the occasion was, no female was allowed any part in the public welcome. A flutter of silks behind the lace curtains, a veiled head peering cautiously through a chink in the door, were all that was to be seen of the womenfolk.

The head of the little community, whose numerous children had at one time or another passed through our hands, invited us to wait in the mosque, and to our amazement allowed us to keep our shoes on. The floor was thickly carpeted and the air heavy with the scent of burning joss sticks, but the room was bare of all ornament, since statues, devotional pictures, ritual objects, have no place in the religion of Islam. A raised settee at one end had been prepared for the honoured guest and was covered with a rich brocade cloth. A few chairs had been provided for western visitors, on which they would be most conspicuous, since the rest of the congregation would sit on the floor.

Out on the pavement the pressmen fidgeted with their cameras, then weary of waiting in the heat, came in to join us. An hour went by, the joss sticks burnt lower and lower. Suddenly there was chattering and laughter, as through a door connecting the mosque with the adjoining house came the girls, most of whom we knew well. Excited and thrilled, they had come to show us the lovely clothes bought in honour of the visit, and the shining jewellery they reserved for special occasions. It was only a fleeting glimpse and our exclamations of pleasure had hardly died away before the whole bright contingent was shepherded back by an agitated mother and never seen again.

Still the leader did not come, and as we whispered together I thought of the generations of Yorkshire-women who had lived in this house, had scrubbed its steps, scoured its sills, and lovingly dusted this very parlour. It was almost impossible to believe that here, where families once sang hymns round the piano on Sunday evenings, the followers of Islam now unrolled their prayer mats and prostrated themselves daily towards Mecca, the cradle of their faith.

All at once cheering and chanting sounded in the street outside and a cloud of rose and marigold petals fluttered through the air. The leader had arrived. Tall and dignified, he looked like an Old Testament prophet, with his snow-white beard and large white pugree.

Graciously and in faultless English he answered the reporters' questions about his faith, explaining the five basic 'pillars' of Islam: belief in one God, ritual prayer five times a day preceded by ablution, almsgiving, the pilgrimage to Mecca, to be made once in a lifetime by every Muslim who could achieve it, and the fast of Ramadhan.

When the interview was over we were glad to leave the now stuffy room for the fresh air outside, where a crowd of men and girls from a nearby mill had gathered in their dinner-hour to see what all the huzzas were about. With a cheerful wave in their direction, the leader walked into the house reserved for the women, from which a few bold little girls had escaped and were running about the street, where the photographers tried eagerly, but in vain, to snap them in their finery. Even the tiny tots knew that they must at all costs avoid the camera, and any who were in doubt about the matter were driven back into the house by the boys, and the doors securely shut and bolted on them.

I had enjoyed the festive occasion and had been made aware, as so often before, of the variety of life in a multi-racial town. Then, as the official car drove away, I caught sight of the great man's wife in the back seat. She was covered from head to toe in a black garment which enveloped her like a shroud. Even her eyes were invisible, for the single slit through which she looked out on the world was veiled with gauze. Suddenly I shuddered in the July sunshine. A shadow had clouded the brightness of the day. The impact of that hooded figure was startling, even painful, and as I walked home I could not forget the sombre vision.

There were times when religious observances made a direct impact on the life of the school. One such occasion was the most important of the Muslim festivals, Ramadhan, the month in which the first revelations of the Koran, the sacred book of Islam, were made known to Mohammed, the Holy Prophet, and throughout which the faithful abstain from food and drink from dawn, 'when the whiteness of the day becomes distinct from the blackness of the night,' until sunset.

To me at least it had never been more than a statement in a diary, *Ramadhan Begins,* but now it became a reality, affecting the lives of children and staff and sometimes the curriculum as well.

During my years of immigrant teaching it fell between December and February, and seemed fated to coincide with the worst weather of the winter or with the Christmas parties. It was impossible not to feel sorry for young people condemned to work through a bitterly cold day without a morsel of food or a comforting hot drink, but they shrugged off our concern and certainly did not want our pity. It was much easier in England than in the Punjab, they told us, for the days were shorter and there was no hot sun to increase their thirst. Since Ramadhan, however, is a movable feast, beginning ten days earlier each year, they will eventually have to endure it in the long days of an English summer.

The lunar month of the fast officially starts when the Imam announces the coming of dawn to the worshippers crowding the mosque. It ends when he declares that the rim of the new moon has appeared above the horizon, but since the exact moment of both these events is difficult to determine in a country where sun and moon may well be hidden by cloud, he is in telephonic contact with two trusted Muslims in Morocco, who confirm that the appointed times have in fact arrived. Those unable to attend prayers at the mosque ring up the Imam to make sure that the fast really has begun or ended.

It was always strictly observed even by our infants, who were under no real obligation to keep the rules, and the more serious-minded boys and girls were keenly aware of its spiritual significance. They understood and appreciated the fact that the disciplines involved were mental and moral as well as physical.

'During Ramadhan,' said Mohammed Latif, 'we must be good, do good and think good,' and in his beautiful decorative script he copied a prayer from the Koran and asked permission to put it up in the cloak-room. He wrote out a blessing for me too.

The stoicism shown by these children, young and old alike, and above all their will-power, won our whole-hearted admiration. Sometimes as the long day wore on they would dearly have loved a drink, but they steadfastly refused both school milk and party feasts until the official hour of sunset had been reached.

At five minutes to four they would sit, straws at the ready, watching the hands of the clock move minute by minute to zero hour. Sometimes there was a hitch in the proceedings, since some followed time-tables specially printed in Bradford, whilst others favoured a Leeds publication or accepted the ruling of a local newspaper. It was all very confusing.

The silence of expectancy would be broken by shrill claims and counter-claims. 'Time!' screamed the Brad-fordians pointing triumphant straws at the clock. 'Not time!' roared the Leodiensians defiantly folding their arms, whilst supporters of Huddersfield or Halifax, secure in the conviction that they alone were right, had already got down to business and were sucking away with grunts of satisfaction.

Towards the end of the fast the children, inevitably, began to show signs of weariness and strain, and work had to be adjusted accordingly. Occasionally one of them would faint and have to be taken home, but any nourishment given to restore him invalidated the whole of that day. 'Whoever is sick,' says the Koran, 'shall

151

fast a like number of other days.' A boy who was un-
thinkingly revived with sal volatile had to abstain for
an extra twelve hours whilst others were celebrating,
because he had inadvertently allowed water to enter
his mouth. Both boys and girls refused to swim in case
they, too, should swallow an offending drop and be
penalised.

When the new moon finally appeared we were bombarded with *Happy Eid* cards and presents of bangles
and beads, for the end of the fasting brought with it a
great celebration called Eid, on the morning of which
the children stayed at home to attend the feasting. 'Our
Christmas,' they called it, and came bouncing back in
the afternoon, gorged and replete, resplendent in new
clothes and shining ornaments. Their half-day holiday
was unofficial, and we turned a blind eye to the mass
absences. They had earned their feast.

Of course, as with all privileges, this one was sometimes abused, especially by one of the most religious
families. The Salaam-I-Not-Comings we called them,
for if we met them in the town on one of their innumerable and illicit days off, they would greet us with
'Salaam! I not coming!' then dive for cover into the
nearest supermarket. Their Eid lasted not for a single
morning but for three whole days, and they were the
bane of the Welfare Officer's existence.

'Not the Salaams again!' he would groan when
asked to visit. 'What is it this time? A week off to cele-
brate yet another new baby, or a fortnight off for the
end of Ramadhan?'

'Well, they're a very religious sect,' I would say to
pacify him. 'They're supposed to be very holy.'

'I wish someone would tell them that cleanliness is

next to holiness,' he used to retort. 'They're one of my few dirty immigrant families, and they're filling their particular street with little Salaams. Not only that, but as I haven't any children of my own they're always offering me one of theirs. 'You want, you take!' says old man Salaam, and the trouble is they're such fetching little so-and-so's that I'm tempted. What my wife would say if I presented her with one I don't know. Well, I do know! She'd say, "It's lovely. But I hope it isn't a Salaam!"'

The second great Muslim festival is the Baqr Eid, the Festival of the Goat, commemorating the story of Abraham and his son, in this case Ishmael, and not Isaac as in the Old Testament version. To all Muslims the day is one of feasting, rejoicing and happiness, and the children stayed away, boys to accompany their fathers to the mosque and girls to help prepare the meal and to dress in their most beautiful clothes.

The offering up of a sacrifice, a camel, a sheep, a goat, was formerly a central part of the festival, but here in England prayers followed by a party seemed to be the order of the day.

Sometimes Indians joined in the celebrations too and once a group of boys, the Bhangra dancers, performed a corn dance, ancient and beautiful, traditional to the Punjab and so the common heritage of both communities. Dressed in white and scarlet and green, with multi-coloured scarves floating from their wrists, they stamped out the primitive rhythm to the insistent beating of a drum, and in dance and mime acted out the cycle of the farmer's year. Yoked pairs of oxen strained at the plough, then brown hands with wide-flung gestures sowed the seed, reaped the grain with a downward sweep of the scythe, and vigorously threshed it. Between every phase of the dance, the boys circled slowly, hands raised above their heads with fingertips touching, to symbolise the growing corn. This was the life they knew, close to the earth, geared to the seasons, to seedtime and growth and harvest, and they danced with passionate concentration. Even those who had been long in England, and only dimly recalled the rich wheatlands which had been their home, seemed stirred by racial memory, and we watched spellbound as the slow ritual unfolded.

Early in November came the Hindu festival of Diwali, or Dipavali, when the people of the Punjab decorate their windows and flat roofs with twinkling oil-lamps, or dipas, to welcome Lakshmi, the Goddess of Wealth, who thus propitiated ensures prosperity for the coming year.

That at least is one explanation of its origin, but different parts of India have different legends. Whatever the truth might be, I heartily approved of the rejoicings and, hoping to enrich the experience of our English children by letting them share in an Indian festival, made plans for a small ceremony within the school. Nightlights in coloured jamjars, burning joss sticks and excited boys and girls in bright eastern dress achieved a little of the atmosphere of a Punjabi village. The children said so.

They set themselves eagerly to entertain us. Sikhs sang of holy gurus, Muslims intoned hymns in honour of the Prophet, and tiny twins piped out a train song complete with whistles. Two handsome Singhs, accompanying themselves on finger-drums, roared out a fighting duet and pulled each other's moustaches in boisterous mime. Little Mukhtar performed back to front because he was too shy to face the audience, and Azam wailed an interminable chant. 'He don't sing very good,' his friends confided in a whisper as he started on the thirty-ninth verse. I had secretly thought so myself.

My job as producer and announcer was no sinecure. 'Now this song,' I would say to the school, 'is in Punjabi, but if you listen carefully you'll hear the sound of a bird, because it's about a cuckoo.' The only cuckoo during that recital was the compère.

'I sang another one,' said Palvinder gleefully as he skipped away to the dressing-room.

To Baisakhi, the Sikh New Year, we were welcomed with the greatest warmth and friendliness by the tall, turbaned men who in physique and bearing could have been the original soldier-saints of Guru Gobind Singh. Strange music played on unfamiliar instruments accompanied the singing of Sikh *shabads,* or hymns, from the holy scriptures. In the talks that followed we learnt something of the Sikh faith, so tolerant of other creeds and one of the few religions which never seeks converts. The doors are wide open to anyone wishing to become a Sikh, but there are no missionaries, no proselytising, no indoctrination or crusades. In the simple sermon with which the ceremony closed, the leader of the temple touched the heart of the matter. 'If you are a Christian, be a good Christian. If you are a Muslim, be a good Muslim. That is all the Sikh asks of you.'

Of the Christian festivals, Harvest Thanksgiving needed least explanation. Sons and daughters of farmers, born and bred on the fertile plains of the Punjab, the children knew all about harvest, though our way of celebrating it was strange to them. Their contributions were generous and varied, bananas and barfi, lemons and laddoo, curry powder and piles of chupattis.

We feared they might find the service tedious, and there was always the chance that the hymns, which they found excruciatingly funny, might trigger off a fit of uncontrollable giggling. 'English singing is all *ee, ee, ee,*' they would say, but shaken by the news that Indian singing sounded just as peculiar to us, they promised not to laugh, and sat quietly through the meaningless ritual. A few minor incidents helped things along. Little Siddiq stuck his head through a wreath of evergreens, where it remained during the whole of the prayer, and in a sudden pause Parvez struck up an Urdu chant of his own, whilst the tiny and the naughty had to be nursed during the sermon, and finished up fast asleep in the arms of the staff.

Differences in religion were more apparent than usual at Christmas. The story of the Nativity was told simply and without comment, as a necessary background for the festivities in which all would join, whatever their race or creed, and they responded with joy to every aspect of the familiar tale. Born and brought up in villages almost as primitive as Bethlehem, they exchanged shrill cries of recognition at the sight of ox and ass beside the manger. 'Lovely cow!' said one little expert gazing wide-eyed at a picture of the stable. 'Lots of milk downstairs!' As for the Christ child, he was completely real and human, for in almost every Asian home there was a baby.

With the older Muslims, however, great diplomacy

was needed to keep the Christmas spirit flowing. It was always made clear that they were not being asked to accept the Christian version of the story, and that no attempt was being made to persuade them to become Christians, for we knew well that while Muslims revere Christ as a prophet from God, they do not believe in his divinity. Herein lay the crux of all the feuds which through the centuries have bedevilled the relationship between Islam and Christianity. For Islam, Mohammed was the last and greatest of the prophets, and Christ was simply one of his predecessors.

There was far less cause to worry about the Sikhs. Since Sikhism is an offshoot, as well as a reform, of Hinduism, it has its same all-embracing qualities, for Hinduism accepts different concepts of God for different levels of humanity. Hence the faith can absorb the peasant who worships an idol as his God, as well as the spiritually gifted guru who sees God as the infinite power in life. Sikhism has inherited this tolerance and, unlike Islam, is not concerned with Christ at all, but with the rules of conduct laid down by its ten holy teachers or gurus.

I always began my explanation simply. 'I am going to tell you the story of the English Christmas,' I would say, 'because I want you to know why English people are happy at this time. Remember, I do not ask *you* to believe this story, but I want you to know why English people believe it, because you are in England now.'

The lesson was usually accepted without demur, but once, when I had taken particular care not to offend any section of the class, Muslim, Sikh or Christian, a Pakistani boy put up his hand. 'Then who was the father of Jesus?' he demanded.

I could have cried. His only reason for asking this vital question was to put me in a difficult position, for he was a born trouble-maker. To Islam it is the ultimate blasphemy even to suggest that God could ever have appeared in human form, and the belief that God is Spirit is inculcated into every Muslim child from its earliest years.

Another Muslim, adept at English, took instant command of the situation. 'You are a silly boy!' he said. 'Miss has told you this story is for Christians. Remember!' he added pointing dramatically to the ceiling. 'There is only one God.'

And the bell rang for playtime.

Sometimes the Christian children had their troubles too. In Class 4, upholding the banner of the West with considerable panache, was Angelo, a bouncing young extrovert from Italy, beaming with goodwill and bursting with initiative, most of it misapplied. His English was fluent but picturesque, and thickly overlaid with Yorkshire. His relations with this Asian class were cordial, almost avuncular. He bossed them, and organised them, and punched them only when he knew it was for their good. Little Tarik adored him. He sharpened his pencils, carried his football boots, sat with his face continually turned towards his idol and laughed uproariously at almost everything he said.

It was on the day the class began to make the Christmas crib that Angelo first became aware of the abyss that yawned beneath his feet. He was issuing orders as usual when, suddenly darting away from the busy group, he grabbed my arm and pushed me into the corridor.

'Cum 'ere, Miss!' he said in a tone which for him

was *sotto voce,* but which from anyone else would have passed for shouting. 'I wants to tell yer sumfink.' His manner was strangely subdued. 'Them in there, Miss!' he hissed, pointing an inky paw at a group who were innocently cutting out the Virgin Mary. 'They're *right bad!*'

'But Angelo!' I protested. 'I thought you liked them. You've always been so happy together.'

'We was, Miss,' he said wistfully, like one looking back to a Golden Age. 'But now they say there isn't a Jesus. That's bad, isn't it, Miss?'

He was on the verge of tears. Devout little Catholic that he was, he felt that the foundations of his world had been shattered. As gently as I could, I told him that the world had many faiths, and that the boys and girls who were his friends worshipped God in ways which were different from his own. It was a staggering shock. 'But it isn't right, Miss!' he insisted, and took a swinging kick at the door in his anguish, then bowing his head he strode manfully back into a pagan world.

Next day he came with his First Communion medal dangling from a white ribbon on his breast. It was obviously intended to create around him a *cordon* not only *sanitaire,* but *catholique* as well. Every now and then he took it off and swung it three times, defiantly, in the direction of a Muslim crony, or whirled it around his head to purify the contaminated air he had unwittingly been compelled to breathe.

Angelo had an ear for music. He loved to sing, loudly of course, for pianissimo was not in his nature, but his voice was tuneful and true. He made up his mind that come what may these heretics should not disgrace him at the carol concert. The fact that Asians are insensitive

159

to the tones and rhythms of western music was a fact he could never understand. 'They doesn't 'alf sing queer, Miss!' he complained, as his comrades droned their way through the morning hymns like bagpipes clogged with grit. Now, a self-appointed maestro, he dragooned his reluctant choristers, rehearsing them at playtime and in the dinner-hour, flailing away with a ruler and shouting, ' 'Orrible! Not right!' above the pipes and squeaks. He drove them so hard that at last even the doting Tarik rebelled.

His *pièce de résistance* was 'Come all ye faithful'. His choir pronounced it 'patepul.' Called in to help with the words, I realised for the very first time that the familiar carol bristled with difficulties not only linguistic but theological. What, I wondered, would Class 4 make of 'begotten not created?' How would good Muslims react to 'now in flesh appearing?' And how, oh how! should we negotiate the Virgin's womb?

'This is difficult for you,' I said. 'We'll just learn the first verse and the chorus.' Both choir and conductor stared at me frankly incredulous.

'All werses!' they shrieked, waving their hymnbooks. 'Every one werse! No missings!'

And that was that. When the East has made up its mind, there is nothing the West can do about it. I began to read aloud.

> God of God, Light of Light,
> Lo! He abhors not the . . .

There was just a chance that I might get away with it. I saw Mohammed Latif beginning to fidget. A determined boy, eager to learn, he had all the tenacity of his race. He would let nothing pass. He was putting his hand up.

'I don't know what is a Wergin,' he moaned, puckering his forehead into lines of worry. 'I don't know what is a voom!'

I pretended not to hear.

'A voom!' he shrilled. 'I don't know what is!'

It was Angelo who saved me. 'Shurrup!' he said with an impatient Latin gesture. 'Ger'on, Miss!' I could have kissed him.

As soon as Christmas preparations were under way, staff began to receive shy offerings of cards. Bought with enthusiasm, presented with affection, they had been chosen indiscriminately from the newsagent's rack and selected for colour rather than content, with the result that we acquired greetings for every occasion, from a silver wedding to the birth of twins. 'Congratulations on your Engagement' said my first. 'Yippee! Now you're 6!' read my second, and 'God Bless your Baby' my third.

Sometimes the cards were old ones, passed on to the children by kindly English neighbours and with the original inscriptions intact. *To Beatrice and George from Evelyn and Albert* was my favourite in this category.

Often the donor, having gravely acknowledged our thanks, would politely ask to have the card back again 'to give to Mr Piper' or some other favourite, and cards which had been admired and exclaimed over on a colleague's desk would mysteriously appear on one's own.

As one room after another broke out in a rash of holly and balloons, excitement began to mount, especially with Class 5, who were restless at the best of times. Decorations went to their heads. In response to cries of,

'Gimmee sticky! Gimmee!' rolls of sellotape flew through the air. Half-completed garlands dangled from lamp-shades. A pathetic little boy who had arrived only that morning had wrapped a handkerchief around his eyes and was swaying to and fro, moaning gently to himself. He was probably praying.

The centrepiece of their grand design was to be a 6ft frieze, with holly in the corners and a border of angels with trumpets, proceeding like Urdu script from right to left. In the middle would be Christmas Father, as the department insisted on calling him. After all, it was perfectly logical. There were Christmas cards, Christmas trees, Christmas parties, so why not Christmas Father? Perhaps because of the Asian respect for old age, he was a general favourite. 'Very laughing!' they would say. 'Very nice old man!'

The cardboard templates had been carefully prepared, and in the simplest of terms Miss had explained the meaning of the various symbols. The class listened with growing impatience. 'We know! We know!' they cried as she held up stars and bells and fir trees. But the angels brought them up standing. There was even a moment of silence as they directed a disbelieving stare at the heavily draped females whose cardboard image she was endeavouring to describe. Then the storm of comment broke.

'Dear me!'

'Why they flying?'

'Very fat!'

'Birds, Miss?' asked one, incredulous. 'In night-dress?'

'No, not birds,' she said firmly. 'Ladies! Good ladies!' Somehow it sounded unconvincing. 'They come from God,' she added lamely. A vista of theological argument too exhausting to contemplate opened suddenly before her, and she moved hastily on to mistletoe.

At this moment an uproar broke out among the chainmakers at the other side of the room. There were piercing shrieks and much wailing of females. A Muslim had hit a Sikh on the head with a gluepot, and the Sikh had punctured the aggressor with a drawing-pin.

By the time peace had been restored in that sector, chaos had overtaken the frieze. Christmas trees hung upside down in the sky with stars nestling in their roots. Bells pealed at impossible angles. There were angels impaled on clumps of holly, but still desperately clutching their instruments, which looked more like sawn-off shotguns than trumpets. There were even halves of angels. Instructions to fold the paper before cutting, and to place the templates to the fold, had been received loud and clear, but not understood, and now a line of seraphs cleft vertically down the middle clawed their way, each on a single pinion, through the over-populated skies. 'Very good work!' said the children when the creation had been fixed somewhat rakishly to the wall, and with undiminished vigour they turned to the manufacture of paper hats.

The following year I decided to strike out and decorate my room with friezes of a more eastern nature and made a set of templates from a book of Indian sculpture. Then, instead of rows of running, jumping, upside-down angels, we had rows of running, jumping, upside-down oriental maidens. They looked wonderfully ornamental and the class wriggled in ecstasy.

The door opened to admit the art master. He looked long and hard at the colourful array, scrutinising each prancing dame with the eye of a connoisseur. Then he addressed the class.

'Well, children!' he said. 'You have worked very hard and made some very, very beautiful pictures.' Coming as it did from a specialist, and from a master they loved to please, this was the ultimate in praise. Twenty faces glowed and twenty beaming smiles met my own.

'But,' he whispered confidentially to me as he turned to go, 'you did know that where they come from only prostitutes dance—or didn't you?'

I had forgotten. I looked in horror from the frieze to the happy faces below and made an instant decision to leave my joyous ladies where they were.

No Asian parents objected when their children were given parts in the Nativity Play, and every year Muslim and Hindu infants stood with the integrated throng around the manger.

A friend in a neighbouring school did once receive a protest from a six-year-old who intimated that a Muslim could not, in conscience, be a Christian shepherd. 'Nonsense!' she said briskly. 'The shepherds weren't Christians!' And that was that.

The smallest were chosen to be angels because they looked so fetching in wings and halo. Very conscious of their high estate, they were inclined to be uppish with the Bethlehem lot, contrasting their own nylon underslips and lace-trimmed waist petticoats with the pyjama bottoms and bits of old curtain in which the shepherds watched their flocks by night. One who looked strangely buxom put his hand into his bosom during a carol which bored him, and drew out a buttered currant muffin, which he ate to the last delicious crumb.

Although the Christmas parties were eagerly anticipated, they were not always enjoyed, though the children had provided most of the fare themselves. Piles of bright iced cakes from Woolworth's rose like coloured islands between the less garish Indian dainties, and down the centre was a mound of fragrant fruit. Thinking to please them we had provided jelly.

'Yelly?' they said shuddering. 'No like!'

'It walking!' said Hamida, shrinking back in horror as it trembled towards her on the plate, and we realised that by some at least its quivering was mistaken for a sign of life. Even by adults, jelly was regarded with suspicion, but for a different reason.

'Please will you tell me!' asked a Hindu mother. 'Is the red, square jelly made of cow's bones?'

It had never occurred to us that a sweet so exclusively associated with fruit could possibly have animal connections, but a jelly baron confirmed her fears. The gelatin used, he wrote, was in fact extracted from ox-bones, so jelly, for her at least, was out.

Among the exotic foods and chain-store biscuits was one lonely meat pie. It lay by itself at the end of the table, regarded with suspicion by all. Yet someone had brought it, and rather than hurt the donor's feelings we cut it into four and tried to hide the portions among the egg sandwiches, but at the end of the feast, there they still were, four passports to perdition, shunned by Sikh and Muslim alike.

When Christmas Father had distributed his gifts, the immemorial East took over. Whilst the English children played happily with the toys they had been given, the sons of Asia huddled in excited groups, heads together, haggling expertly with each other, and driving a hard bargain as they traded a false moustache for a packet of balloons, a tractor for a whistle, and anything on earth for a bag of marbles. It was safe to assume that by four o'clock not a single gift would remain in the hands of its original owner.

The activities of Christmas Father were far more difficult to explain than the simple story of the Nativity. We dreaded the question, 'Will he come down our chimenee, or does he only come down English chimenees?' for it was one we could not honestly answer. If he failed to leave presents at their homes, and there was no reason to suppose that he would, bright hopes which we alone had raised would remain cruelly unfulfilled. In that case, was it fair to tell the younger children about him at all? Yet he was inescapable. Representations of him were all about them, and they needed to know why we were all so fond of our red-cheeked, white-bearded guru. Should the seniors, then, be let into the secret that he was only father in a dressing-gown, or worse still just mother, not dressed up at all?

It was a dilemma we never successfully resolved. The fact that they received gifts at their own great festivals, the Sikh New Year, the Muslim Eid, did not compensate for a bitter disappointment at Christmas, and realising this, a wise family here and there would conform to English custom purely for the sake of the children.

If religious festivals, whether Sikh, Muslim or Christian, were shared and enjoyed by members of all the communities, so too were more secular occasions, chief among them 'Indian pictures.'

Every group of expatriates has its social centre, its communal meeting-place where for the hour at least it can be truly itself, natural, uninhibited, nostalgic, free from the strain of keeping up appearances in a foreign land. For the Indians and Pakistanis in our town it was the cinema, rented for the whole of every Sunday and crammed to the last plush seat with families eager for a glimpse of home.

'You coming to Indian pictures?' the children would ask, waving the illustrated leaflet which gave details of the next performance. 'Very good fillum, this one. Lots of fighting. Many robbers.' When we promised to go, they were overjoyed. 'Look for me,' they would say. 'I'll tell you all what happens.'

We never needed to look for them. The news of our arrival, semaphored from the foyer to the audience within, brought the children hurtling out to see if it was true, and to escort us down the aisle in an excited bunch.

In spite of my ignorance of Urdu, Hindi or Punjabi, I always enjoyed the day's entertainment, even if the vagaries of the plot, and they were many, escaped me. It seemed that the heroine, always a poor village girl, had to suffer incredible hardships before finally getting her man. I have seen her trapped in a burning house, thrown into a pit of lions, chopped down with an axe and swept away in a flood, all in the same film. Yet miraculously, without any visual explanation, she always turned up in the next shot singing and dancing as if her life were one long musical comedy.

These carefree interludes, the beautiful village

dances, the lilting love duets, had nothing to do with the plot, but always seemed to follow the most harrowing tragedies, perhaps because so much suffering could not be borne without a little light relief. The death of a beloved husband, or the mere amputation of his arms and legs, never deterred the entire cast from erupting into song.

The anti-heroine, easily recognisable by her permed hair and western clothes, always prospered until the very end, when she vanished without trace, whereas the villain, usually fat and old and the village money-lender, underwent a sudden transformation and became the village clown. This lewd old man, who for three-quarters of the film had leered and lusted after the simple village girl, and had cheated her family out of their money in order to win her, never received his just deserts. He finished up either sitting in the river covered with mud, or with a pot of paint upside down on his head in the best slapstick tradition.

Most surprising was the emphasis on romantic love, since in both India and Pakistan the arranged marriage is the rule and not the exception. It was easy to identify the lovers. If a man hurled a woman playfully about, it was a good sign. If he chased her through the cornfields to the accompaniment of joyful lyrics and a threepiece band it was definite proof of their affection.

Of course there was never anything indelicate, even when passion was on the boil. The camera would linger first on one adoring face then on the other, but never on both at the same time, for any love-making between actor and actress was completely taboo. The lips that yearned across the screen met only celluloid. Once, the couple almost held hands, and I felt the tension mounting in the audience. Would or wouldn't their fingers actually meet? The suspense was agonising. I, too, was on the edge of my seat with excitement. They didn't! And the whole cinema relaxed into embarrassed laughter. It had been a very close thing! Rumour has it that in more modern films the couple actually kiss, but I cannot bring myself to believe it.

Sometimes in the older films there were lapses in continuity. I have seen the heroine's costume change colour in the middle of a dance, and a bowl of roses transform itself into a jug of marigolds, but what the productions lacked in quality they more than made up for in quantity. All lasted for at least three hours and contained enough plots and subplots for a dozen films or even a television serial. One reel before the end the producer seemed to realise that he had hardly any celluloid left, so that suddenly every problem was solved to make way for the happy ending. Villains were killed off and their sidekicks disappeared. The hero received lots of money from who knew where, and the heroine was resurrected from her last, or what I had believed to be her last resting place. All was thus resolved in the last five minutes, the time chosen by the proprietor to stop the film and project the attraction for the following week, to a chorus of boos and catcalls from his thwarted patrons.

I should of course have grasped the plot more effectively if my young interpreters had been more sensitive to my needs. They started enthusiastically enough, but either became so engrossed in the film that they forgot their task altogether, or had not enough English to do the job properly.

'Is that her brother, or her father, or her betrothed?'

I would ask. After all, it made a vital difference to the story.

'*I* don't know!' little Paramjit would answer indignantly, and in a tone which implied that my query was unreasonable.

But later, when the heroine, as even I could see, was threading a needle, Paramjit, anxious to reinstate herself as my official interpreter, would tap me urgently on the shoulder. 'She is threading a needle,' she would inform me. 'Very nice!'

In all the films, incongruous in that exotic setting, were visual reminders of the British Raj, an aspidistra in a Victorian monstrosity of a pot, a knitted teacosy, a crocheted antimacassar, a long-cased mahogany clock on the wall, the flotsam of an empire, all looking strangely forlorn, as if they knew that history had left them stranded.

Even if the melodrama had been wholly incomprehensible I should still have enjoyed the audience. Our children and their families had come for the day, bringing sweets and laddoo and crackling packets of 'crips.' Babies slept, cried, had their feeds and dropped their bottles, which rolled rattling from the back stalls to the front. Little ones staggered to and fro swigging milk or pop, and sat down suddenly in the aisles, where relatives fell over them on their way to the toilets. Toddlers played in the exits and bashed each other with superfluous chupattis. It was very cheerful, very noisy—and very Indian.

The end of the adventure

Time brought great changes to the department. Slowly, inexorably, numbers crept up. Children were having to be pushed out to local schools long before they were ready. From the point of view of integration there were just not enough English boys and girls to go round, to play with, to work with, to talk to. The school was becoming known as 'the immigrant school.' 'Have you any English children there at all?' friends would ask quite seriously, and the original anxiety of parents that their sons and daughters would be handicapped, especially at the eleven-plus stage, by the presence of so many Asians, began to revive and to find public expression.

It was therefore decided to open a separate Reception Centre for children newly arrived from India and Pakistan. There Asian teachers would give them basic social training, and a small English staff would begin simple language work. In addition, every child would be examined by the School Medical Officer and would not be allowed to leave until declared medically fit. In groups of from fifteen to eighteen the children would then be sent out to begin a graded English course, first to schools in their own area, then when those had their quota to schools elsewhere.

The new plan, as all were aware, had disadvantages. Asian parents, naturally enough, could not understand why their children had to travel to a distant school when there was a perfectly good one on their doorstep. Some English parents were disturbed at the prospect of Asian children appearing in 'select' areas of the town, and a number of head teachers at the receiving end were equally unenthusiastic, especially in those same middle-class suburbs. To many educationalists, and to outsiders concerned about race relations, the scheme looked suspiciously like segregation.

Yet the alternative, the concentration of large numbers of non-English speaking children in the one school in their own area, was even more undesirable, for they would then play and work together, speaking Punjabi, with little incentive to learn English. In such a community, too, the English pupils would suffer socially as well as educationally. Being a small minority, they would inevitably feel swamped, and the imbalance would certainly increase racial tension. Our dispersal scheme would, we felt, benefit both races. English children in all parts of the town would discover that people of a different race were not creatures from outer space, and would learn to live with them, to work with them and to accept them. Many were delighted at the novelty of boys with plaits and top-knots and girls in satin trousers. 'Please can we have some more?' a deputation of juniors begged one headmaster. 'We want one each to play with and there aren't enough to go round.' The five-year-olds, in particular, were welcomed almost everywhere, and their appealing ways did more for the cause of race relations than a dozen well-meaning committees.

That Asian boys and girls were segregated in the Reception Centre could not be denied, but their stay was limited, and the weeks they spent there gave them time to settle down. The segregation was linguistic, not racial, and was no different in kind from that applied to children handicapped by blindness, deafness or physical deformity. Our children too, though in a different way, were handicapped.

The complicated business of dispersal was handled by the Education Authority. When a group was ready to leave, the Staffing Officer looked around for a school with an empty classroom, then for a teacher, English or Asian. When he had found both, the Immigrant Welfare Officer looked around for a bus, not always readily available, then planned the operation with military precision. First he chose points at which the children could be safely collected in the morning and deposited again at four o'clock. Then he did his best to explain the plan to parents who knew little or no English, who were not well acquainted with the district and had only a vague sense of time.

Next we took over. In English, Urdu and Punjabi we drilled the children, making sure they knew the time and stopping-place of their bus, the name of their new school and the amount of dinner money they would need on the first morning. Each was given a cardboard ticket with all these details printed on it, and the seniors were told the colour of their new school uniform and where it could be bought.

Morning after morning we saw the Immigrant Welfare Officer dashing round the route in his little car, making sure that the right children were waiting at the right place at the right time. He seemed to be everywhere. Sometimes he was standing at a street corner surrounded by infants. Sometimes he was issuing orders from the platform of the bus, quelling the high-pitched shrieks and shouts with a single penetrating bellow, or upholding the authority of an ex-conjuror who, in the role of escort, needed all his ancient cunning to keep his tinier clients from vanishing under the seats.

If I had doubts about the new plan, the children had none, for a special bus ticket became a status symbol. As the loaded double-deckers lurched out into the suburbs, the élite would wave condescendingly to a once revered, but now passé teacher, or smirk in front of the untouchables who still attended the Centre and went there ignominiously on foot. Every time I passed one of their dragooned queues, for a self-appointed marshal always seemed to line the children up according to size, I was greeted by waving arms and cheerful voices calling, 'Hello! Hello! We're going on the school bus.'

These youngsters were on their way not only to new schools but to a wider experience. They would grow up with English children, seeing, sharing and accepting their way of life, and in that they were more fortunate than their adolescent brothers and sisters. Life in a permissive England was difficult for young people who were accustomed to strict family discipline, and who had little or no voice in decisions affecting their future. They had come at a time when the gap between their traditional values and those of their adopted country could hardly have been wider, and the strain of living between the two worlds was more keenly felt by girls than by boys.

Whilst their English friends chose their own clothes, experimented with hair styles and followed every exciting trend of fashion, Asian teenage girls found themselves restricted, apparently for ever, to shalwar and kameez. Even those who had worn uniform at school had to revert to Punjabi dress as soon as they left. Here and there, however, one more wilful than the rest would surreptitiously cut a new kameez to hug the figure, or narrow her shalwar, or flare them slightly at the ankles. 'My big sister, she's got belly bottoms,' reported Resham, proud to be related to such sophistication. Few succumbed to the skirt, mini, midi or maxi.

Two Indian girls, both students, who had completely westernised their dress, had to face hostility and taunts from their womenfolk.

'They shout at us in the streets,' said one. 'They call out, "Cover up your legs!" and "You are a bad girl!"'

'They call me dirty names,' said the other, 'but I try not to take any notice. There are only two of us at the Tech, and we want to be like the others there.'

'What do you do about uniform?' I asked another Indian girl who was a nurse.

'Oh, I wear it all,' she answered, 'but I take the black stockings and uniform off on the train. I always change into shalwar and kameez before I get here.'

'I see,' I said. 'I suppose some of the women here would shout at you.'

'Oh, yes! They would.' she replied. 'I don't really mind that, but, you see, when I've gone they take it out of my mother, so for her sake I don't wear English dress or uniform at home.'

Boys, on the other hand, were not restricted in any way. They were allowed not only to compromise with, but to copy, the dress of English teenage boys, and their suits were of the smartest cut and the very latest styling.

So strong were the conventions limiting the activities of women to the family circle that few older girls, whether Sikh or Muslim, had any chance of pursuing hobbies or interests outside the home. So many simple pleasures were denied them, so much that to us seemed innocent enjoyment was regarded as sinful by their elders, that their lives continued to be almost as circumscribed as in their Punjabi village. Youth Clubs where both sexes met for dancing or amateur dramatics were absolutely taboo, since no respectable girl could ever make an exhibition of herself on a stage, and dancing, except in private, was beyond the pale. The few girls who, reluctantly and after much passionate pleading, had been allowed to join the Girl Guides, were soon stopped from attending because the meetings went on until nine o'clock, far too late for them to be out by themselves.

Yet boys were allowed out alone and late at night, so could if they wished to join Youth Clubs, even the ATC or the YMCA and those who played in school teams were able to meet English boys of their own age, and at matches and as spectators had every opportunity of making friends.

When most girls left school their education came to a full stop. Jagindro wanted desperately to be a nurse, but father would not hear of it, so Jagindro stayed at home and helped to look after the babies and cook chupattis until she was old enough to look after her own babies and cook her own chupattis. Mussarat, who wanted to be 'a reading-writing lady,' was more fortunate and was allowed to stay on into the Sixth Form.

The situation has, however, eased a little in recent years. Some girls are going out to work in mills, factories and tailoring establishments before they marry. The discovery by their menfolk that women can be an economic asset, and can contribute substantially to the family budget, may yet break down the prejudice of centuries.

Boys for the most part followed the same occupations as their fathers, spinning and weaving in the woollen mills, working in foundries or public transport. More recently a few have been placed as apprentices. One who came to me as a five-year-old is training to be a TV engineer, whilst another is an apprentice mechanic at a garage. At present only a small percentage are continuing their education into the Sixth Form or at a College of Technology. The O-Level, and even the A-Level results published in the local paper are beginning to include a sprinkling of Asian names, though passes have been gained in only one or two subjects, but at least they are there.

It was taken for granted that girls would marry, for spinsterhood is almost unknown in Asia. It was a cause of real distress to our infants that their Miss was single. Puzzled and unhappy, they discussed the matter endlessly amongst themselves. She was not in any way deformed, she had the requisite number of arms and legs, her breath was sweet, especially when they had

plied her with pumpkin seeds, and she was not notice-
ably ill-favoured—but she had no husband. Again and
again they asked her, 'You not married, Miss?' hoping
they had misunderstood or had perhaps been misin-
formed.

An inadequate dowry, they decided, could be the
only reason for her plight, and in a frenzy of compensation they loaded her with plasticine wedding rings and
pressed plasticine marriage ornaments on her forehead.
'*Now* you married, Miss!' they cried, dancing with
satisfaction, as tugging and pulling at her skirt they led
her to the cloakroom mirror.

In all their young lives they had never met or heard
of an unmarried woman who lived alone. 'Nobody in
house?' they exclaimed, their eyes wide with pity.
'Only you?' and were not comforted when she told
them that she had two lovely cats to keep her company.
Little Sharifa came next day with an old brass curtain
ring, and pushed it on to her finger. 'A wedding man,'
she said firmly, 'is nicer than cats, Miss.'

Boys and girls were often betrothed at an early age
and even one of our six-year-olds had achieved the
status of a fiancé.

'What's the name of your betrothed?' we asked him.

'Jasbinder,' he piped.

'What's she like?'

'*I* don't know,' he answered indifferently, and far
more interested in his jigsaw. 'I never seen her.'

Both boys and girls will have to face the fact that
their marriage will be an arranged one, and as yet the
majority are perfectly content to follow the custom of
centuries and to leave the choice of a partner entirely
to their parents.

'It works,' said sixteen-year-old Paramjit, a determined young lady with a mind of her own.

'But what happens if you don't like him?' I asked.

'You're just stuck with him!' she replied with an engaging grin, but the prospect seemed to hold no terrors. 'You can say no, but you never do.'

As long as the girls are part of a society in which the parents' right to choose is accepted unreservedly by all, the system seems at least as successful as the free-for-all taken for granted in England. Though it saddened us at first, we came to see that it had advantages. For Asian girls, the ever-increasing pressure to be popular with the opposite sex and to have a boy friend at an ever earlier age does not exist, and the stress and strain of adolescence are far less acutely felt. They are free to enjoy their youth secure in the knowledge that one day they will marry, marriage being not a personal achievement but a natural part of the life cycle, birth, childhood, adolescence, marriage, motherhood and death.

The marriage, once contracted, begins with much in its favour. Since parents on either side are unlikely to level criticism at a son- or daughter-in-law they have carefully selected themselves, trouble with in-laws is reduced to a minimum. Nor can discord arise from differences in religion or social background, since matches are made to ensure harmony on these points, and though there is still room for the unexpected hitch, a number of obstacles are thus removed before ever the wedding takes place.

That a girl will grow to love her husband is to them as natural, as self-evident as that a child will grow to love its parents, though in neither case has free choice entered into the matter. A union contracted without parental consent is a family disgrace. Only the children who are born here, who grow to maturity within the framework of our freer society, enjoying the benefits of our equal and liberal education, will find difficulty in accepting the age-old custom. The young people who suffer most will not be those who fully acquiesce, nor those who have the courage fully to reject, but those who, having seen a different way of life, are still bound to the old by a tie so strong that they cannot bring themselves to break it.

Already there are rebels among them. One boy told me frankly that he went out with English girls and wanted to choose his own bride. Another, betrothed from boyhood to a girl in India, had his engagement broken off when a neighbour wrote to her father reporting that he was friendly with English girls. One outstandingly brave Muslim girl has married the boy of her choice in spite of bitter and prolonged opposition from her family. Faintly the pattern of the future is beginning to emerge, and parents would do well to ponder the inscription BASHIR LOVE WITH GIRL scribbled in chalk on a local hoarding. The writing is quite literally on the wall!

Kulwant, the first of my pupils to be married, invited me to her wedding at the Sikh Temple, a large Victorian house which had recently been converted. The entrance hall was full of shoes, shoes of every conceivable type, from sharply pointed chukka boots, size ten, to glamorous golden-thonged sandals in a dainty three. Leaving my own size fives, I followed Gudi, my young guide, up the stairs and into the main room of the temple. It was bright with colour and pungent with the smell of burning joss-sticks. Eastern music, strangely hypnotic, throbbed in my ears, and soft carpets pandered to my feet.

The room, devoid of furniture, was dominated by a huge silken canopy, decorated with ribbons and glittering baubles, and beneath it, on a small raised stand, was the *Granth Sahib*. Gudi went quietly to the front and bowed her head in reverence. I followed and then joined the women huddled on the floor.

I soon found the bride. Her outfit was delightful. A bright red and gold embroidered tunic topped her red satin trousers. Around her head and shoulders was a red velvet scarf edged with gold, and draped over this, disclosing only the merest tip of her nose, was a red gauzy veil.

'Show her your presents,' urged Gudi, and Kulwant at last showed signs of life. Pulling aside her veil and grinning broadly, she proudly displayed beautiful bracelets, necklaces and rings of soft, bright Indian gold, as well as a pink bri-nylon cardigan, her one concession to western civilisation.

At this point we were joined by three of her friends from the factory. 'Me mates!' said Kulwant by way of introduction. Mascara-ed, mini-skirted, bare-headed, they created a sensation!

The men, seated at the opposite side of the room, were not all the bearded Sikhs of romantic fiction, for some were clean-shaven, and wore white knotted handkerchiefs over their mod haircuts. I wondered which of them was destined for Kulwant, for neither she nor I had seen the bridegroom before, and I felt a pang of sympathy for this young girl, who was soon to commit herself for life to a complete stranger. Suddenly the girls around her began to twitter like excited sparrows. The groom's party had arrived. Only Kulwant remained calm and aloof.

'Which one is he?' asked one of the mates.

'That's him! That's him!' exclaimed Gudi.

And there he was, tall and darkly handsome. He wore a pale pink turban, and a garland of flowers around his neck. The ceremony began. A tall, distinguished Sikh with twirling grey whiskers, blue turban and a smartly-cut suit began to intone prayers in which the congregation joined as if in response, then Kulwant was taken by her mother to the front of the canopy, where she knelt modestly beside her betrothed.

I could not understand the ceremony. I knew that the emphasis in a Sikh marriage was placed upon the joining of two minds and of two souls. I knew that the coconut wrapped in a long white towel carried by the groom was a symbol of purity, but that was all I knew. Four times the bridal pair left their kneeling position and made a circuit of the canopy whilst we showered them with crumpled rose petals. On the fourth and final circuit Kulwant shyly took hold of one end of the towel, and the congregation seemed to relax.

'First time round she no hold,' said Gudi. 'Two and three times round she no hold. But four times round she hold. Then she married.'

There followed more singing from a small choir of men, then the relatives of the pair went in turn to the dais and with graceful gestures circled the bowed heads of the bridal couple with pound notes, which they then laid reverently before them.

I had entered the temple with thoughts full of sadness for Kulwant and this strange, loveless marriage, but by the end of the ceremony my doubts were dispelled. I knew in my heart that for her all would be well, but for her children and her grandchildren, torn between the customs of East and West as they would surely be, I felt no such certainty. For them, a wedding might not be the happy, memorable occasion that this one, at least, had been for me.

Jaswant and Jasbiro, some months later, accepted their unknown bridegrooms with equal composure. Both produced babies with commendable speed and were obviously happy. Jasbiro told me that she intended to have another baby later, but no more.

'One or two babies,' she said, 'eats nice, dresses nice. But too many babies, we don't eat or dress nice.' Short though it had been, her sojourn in the West had taught her an important economic truth.

But there were other girls who came back to tell me of their approaching marriage with no joy at all.

'Oh Miss!' said one. 'I am very frightened.'

'What are you frightened of?' I asked as gently as I could. 'Are you frightened of your husband, or frightened of having a baby?'

'I am frightened of everything,' was her quiet despairing reply.

When a shy Pakistani sixteen-year-old was told that a marriage had been planned for her, and that soon she would be going to live in the Midlands, far away from everyone she knew, she burst into a storm of weeping. 'She cry for two weeks,' reported her younger sister. 'She never stop. She says she doesn't want to get married.' My heart ached for her, so timid, so withdrawn, so afraid of life, and I felt then that in spite of the advantages an eastern marriage might have, it must still be a shock for a shy and sensitive girl to share both her bed and her body with a stranger.

Before the seniors left us, we attempted to explain the patterns and values of the society into which they had been plunged. It had to be made clear that here in the West the position of women was profoundly different from that to which they were accustomed, a point readily understood by the Indian boys, for India, after all, has a woman Prime Minister, and for centuries Sikh women have enjoyed greater freedom than their Muslim sisters.

With the Muslim boys, however, any suggestion that woman was the equal of man, that she had any status in society other than that of wife, mother, cook and handmaid, was received with polite incredulity. It seemed to us that on this point the adherents of Islam were more harsh than their great founder, who declared that women must be held in respect, and who even allowed them certain legal rights.

Whilst women from educated families did, in fact, enjoy these privileges, with simple village people the gulf between precept and practice was immense. Some Pakistani mothers lived in near-purdah, and sometimes we would see a curtain cautiously moved aside to give a glimpse of a hooded figure peering, half curious, half afraid, at the world outside.

Even young Pakistani boys vaunted their male superiority, and the smallest of infants would show a frightening disdain for their mothers. We often pitied older sisters saddled with the responsibility of looking after these diminutive despots, but they meekly and without a murmur accepted inferiority as their lot.

'Boys first! Boys first!' the infants would shout as they hurled themselves to the front of the dinner queue, and were astounded to learn that in England ladies and girls came first, and should be treated with courtesy and respect. 'You open the door for a lady, carry her shopping bag and bring her a chair,' we told them, and for once they were shocked into silence.

There were senior Pakistani boys who could scarcely conceal their contempt for women teachers. If their English was good enough they would devise cunning test questions, usually mathematical, and spring them on us at inconvenient moments. 'What is twelve times fifty nine?' they would ask. 'You tell me!' or 'Name me a metal!' and wait smugly for the wrong answer, but with patience and good humour their prejudices could usually be overcome.

The strain of living with two irreconcilable standards of conduct must have been considerable. Many of their mothers were not allowed out without a male escort and were expected to walk behind him, whilst all of them wore garments which covered everything except hands and face. Their women teachers, on the other hand, free to walk abroad with anyone they pleased, mini-skirted, hatless, made-up, had to be treated with respect. Yet in spite of this dilemma, the majority of Asian boys treated us with courtesy and never applied their own strict standards to us. It was a situation which must have hurt their womenfolk immensely.

Contacts with English girls of their own age could so easily be unfortunate if Asian boys failed to understand the difference in upbringing between young people from East and West, and we tried to make them see that although English girls showed their legs,

185

bared their arms and used cosmetics, they were not necessarily immoral, a mistake often made by mature Pakistanis.

We had to help them, too, to face colour prejudice. In the sheltered community we had created for them it was seldom apparent. There were no anti-racial slogans chalked on walls, no ugly incidents in the play-ground, yet from time to time a chance remark be-trayed the presence of prejudice, and betrayed, too, the fact that it had originated with parents.

'My Dad's taking me away from this school,' said a five-year-old. 'He doesn't want me to grow up with Nig Nogs.'

'I say,' whispered another, rolling his eyes in amaze-ment at the sight of my all-Asian class. 'Do you only teach Wogs, then?'

A junior who had been to Bradford came back chant-ing a rhyme which showed that race had entered the world of children's folk-lore.

> Lumb Lane! Lumb Lane!
> With rags instead of window pane.
> Where they sleep twelve in a bed,
> And live on Kit-e-Kat and bread.

In the harder world outside school, dislike and dis-crimination were stronger, they were unpleasant, and they hurt. To pretend otherwise would have been dis-honest. I told the children that many disliked them simply because they were Indian or Pakistani. I begged them not to listen to the name-calling, not to retaliate, and to remember that the people who were most hostile were those who knew nothing about them. 'You must show them how friendly Indians and Pakistanis can be,' I would say. 'Always be pleasant and polite. Be proud of being an Indian or a Pakistani.'

I reminded them, too, of some Asian customs which would certainly invite criticism. I warned them that they would invite laughter and contempt if they walked hand in hand with male friends, customs which to them were natural, and I told them of the revulsion felt here at the widespread practice of spitting, a habit which in mills and workshops has done harm to the reputation of immigrant workers. I never knew how much they understood, or even if I was saying the right thing, but those were the best 'adwices' I could give.

The prejudice they encountered was rarely violent, though in some schools there were occasional bouts of fisticuffs between English and Asians. Ill-feeling was more likely to be expressed verbally than physically. A gentle Hindu boy told me he went home for dinner though the distance was considerable, because the walk was preferable to the abuse he had to face from English boys in the school yard. 'They call me a stinking Wog,' he said.

Kamla, a beautiful Muslim girl, as English in her ways as her classmates, came back to see me a few weeks after she had left. 'I don't like it,' she said. 'They call me Baggy Pants, and then they all shout, "Go back where you came from!" ' Her eyes filled with tears. She was shy and sensitive, a child it would seem impossible to dislike.

Some prejudice took more insidious forms. Jasbir, a clever boy in the Sixth Form of a school where immigrants were accepted with more sympathy and tolerance than in many of its kind, had gained seven O-Levels, was courteous and helpful and spoke excellent English, yet he knew he was not wanted.

'Not even you?' I asked, astonished, for he was a prefect and good at games.

'Not even me!' he said smiling. 'I'm as English as you are, but they just don't want to know. Oh, they'll speak to me in classtime—if they have to—but beyond that I don't exist. They stay with their friends and I stay with mine.'

Tolerated but not welcomed, accepted in school and occasionally included in an unofficial game of football in the park, rarely if ever invited to share in leisuretime pursuits or amusements, this, it seemed, was as far as integration could go. Not very encouraging, but it could have been worse.

Prejudice there undoubtedly was in the minds of some of their new teachers too, and though many did their best to hide it, the children sensed that it was there. Sometimes even the five-year-olds, lovable and attractive though they were, had a chilly reception, and how could anyone prepare such babies to meet injustice and hostility? 'Keep your children away from me,' said one young head to their Indian teacher. 'They smell!'

Yet prejudice was not all on one side. Many Pakistanis were haunted by the fear that their own young people would succumb to western fashions and to a way of life which could lead only to hell, and apprehensive fathers married off their daughters at a much earlier age than they would have done in Pakistan, determined that they should achieve marriage before corruption set in.

The majority did not want integration in the fullest sense of the word. Like all national groups in exile, they clung more tenaciously than ever to their customs, both social and religious, and to their traditional dress. They bought their own food from their own shops, and were determined to preserve their way of life, even when it clashed most violently with the requirements of English schools and academic training, or inflamed public sentiment in such matters as the ritual slaughter of animals.

They were bitterly opposed to intermarriage. 'How would you like your daughter to marry one?' is the Englishman's instant query when the immigrant question is raised. His triumphant 'Got-you-there!' look implies that as far as he is concerned there is no more to be said. He has no conception of the horror with which a Pakistani father would greet the announcement that his son was to become engaged to *his* English daughter!

To the general public, racial hostility is a question of black and white. It was therefore astonishing to find that among our small clients the strongest antipathy was that of brown to black. Even an infant Indian or Pakistani might resolutely refuse to hold a Jamaican hand in a ring game, or to walk with a West Indian in a crocodile. 'Me no like!' he would say, stubbornly thrusting his fists into his pockets.

The older children were even more vocal in their objections. When Habhajan had at long last been moved into the main school, his first comments were far from favourable. 'I have to sit next to Winston,' he moaned. 'He's a Jameecan. Too much black!'

But it was Hardial who, in his own inimitable way, put their feelings in a nutshell.

'Oh dear! Oh dear!' he began as usual. 'Our house

is full of knickers. Knickers upstairs and knickers down-stairs. Everywhere knickers!'

'Knickers?' I repeated, puzzled. 'There are knickers all over your house?'

'Yes,' he said earnestly, 'and next door as well. You know!' he added, sensing my utter mystification. 'Knickers! Jameecans!'

Their aversion did not, apparently, prevent them from taking in West Indian lodgers or from accepting them as tenants of their property.

The reasons for the deep-seated dislike were complex and in part historical, for a pale skin, in India, is associated with beauty, and in some parts of the sub-continent a dark countenance carries with it the faint stigma of a primitive culture, associated as it is with the aboriginal inhabitants, the non-Ayran Dravidians, who were mostly dark-skinned.

When at last children were ready to leave us, the final dispersal was always sad. The girls, and even some of the boys, wept unashamedly. Whilst the main school hurtled homewards our children lingered on, reluctant to say a last goodbye. Although from the first it had been their ambition to move into an English school, they were apprehensive now that the moment had come, aware of the enormity of the step they were taking. With us they had been safe and sheltered. Now they would have to make their own way in a harsher and more critical world.

'Please give us your advices,' said Resham as he wrung my hand for the very last time. 'I don't want to go without your advices.'

'We'll come back to see you,' they called as they moved down the yard in forlorn little groups. It was a promise they kept—often.

Again and again they came back, creeping quietly in to listen to a story, or joining in our activities as if they had never been away. It was heart-warming, but it was also disturbing, for it would have been more natural for them to grow away from their primary school as even the most loyal English children do, and should.

'Do you know what we do in the dinner-hour?' Mumtaz asked me during one of her frequent visits. 'We get together in a group and talk about what we did here in our old school.' We should have been better pleased to hear that they were joining in the life of their new school instead.

At times we wondered uneasily if we had cushioned them too much, if by sheltering them from unkindness and prejudice we had in fact done them a disservice, and made it harder for them to adjust to a society which would persistently regard them as aliens. With us they knew that they were welcome, and in the friendly affectionate atmosphere we had tried so hard to create they had found happiness and security, for a time at least.

They had come to us dejected and miserable, their faces blank and uncomprehending, their eyes expressionless. By the time they left us they were moving confidently about the school, assured, independent, tackling jobs, helping the younger ones to settle down and even chatting to each other in the broad, strong accents of the town. 'Shurrup! Give over! Gerraway! Get lost!' were always good to hear, for though not to be found in the textbooks, they meant that our work was done.

It had been hard but infinitely rewarding. We had

learnt to understand customs different from our own, we had become acquainted with two of the world's great religions, and had seen an eastern way of life without ever leaving home.

Most of all, we had enjoyed the children, their humour and their friendliness. It would be easy, almost too easy, to be romantic about them. There were times when we became so involved that we longed to fight all their battles, real or imaginary, but there were others when we despaired of ever understanding them, and when they irritated, even infuriated us because they were so different. Yet in spite of every difficulty and misunderstanding, the years during which they delighted us, provoked us, exasperated and charmed us, were rich in laughter and experience.

TITLES IN THE NEW WINDMILL SERIES

Erik Haugaard: *The Little Fishes*
Esther Hautzig: *The Endless Steppe*
Bessie Head: *When Rain Clouds Gather*
Ernest Hemingway: *The Old Man and the Sea*
John Hersey: *A Single Pebble*
Nigel Hinton: *Getting Free; Buddy*
Alfred Hitchcock: *Sinister Spies*
C. Walter Hodges: *The Overland Launch*
Geoffrey Household: *Rogue Male; A Rough Shoot; Prisoner of the Indies; Escape into Daylight*
Fred Hoyle: *The Black Cloud*
Irene Hunt: *Across Five Aprils*
Henry James: *Washington Square*
Josephine Kamm: *Young Mother; Out of Step; Where Do We Go From Here?; The Starting Point*
Erich Kästner: *Emil and the Detectives; Lottie and Lisa*
M. E. Kerr: *Dinky Hocker Shoots Smack!; Gentlehands*
Clive King: *Me and My Million*
John Knowles: *A Separate Peace*
Marghanita Laski: *Little Boy Lost*
D. H. Lawrence: *Sea and Sardinia; The Fox* and *The Virgin and the Gypsy; Selected Tales*
Harper Lee: *To Kill a Mockingbird*
Laurie Lee: *As I Walked Out One Mid-Summer Morning*
Ursula Le Guin: *A Wizard of Earthsea; The Tombs of Atuan; The Farthest Shore; A Very Long Way from Anywhere Else*
Doris Lessing: *The Grass is Singing*
C. Day Lewis: *The Otterbury Incident*
Lorna Lewis: *Leonardo the Inventor*
Martin Lindsay: *The Epic of Captain Scott*
David Line: *Run for Your Life; Mike and Me; Under Plum Lake*
Kathleen Lines: *The House of the Nightmare; The Haunted and the Haunters*
Joan Lingard: *Across the Barricades; Into Exile; The Clearance; The File on Fräuline Berg*
Penelope Lively: *The Ghost of Thomas Kempe*
Jack London: *The Call of the Wild; White Fang*
Carson McCullers: *The Member of the Wedding*
Lee McGiffen: *On the Trail to Sacramento*
Wolf Mankowitz: *A Kid for Two Farthings*
Olivia Manning: *The Play Room*
Jan Mark: *Thunder and Lightnings; Under the Autumn Garden*
James Vance Marshall: *A River Ran Out of Eden; Walkabout; My Boy John that Went to Sea; A Walk to the Hills of the Dreamtime*
David Martin: *The Cabby's Daughter*
J. P. Martin: *Uncle*
John Masefield: *The Bird of Dawning; The Midnight Folk; The Box of Delights*
W. Somerset Maugham: *The Kite and Other Stories*
Guy de Maupassant: *Prisoners of War and Other Stories*
Laurence Meynell: *Builder and Dreamer*
Yvonne Mitchell: *Cathy Away*
Honoré Morrow: *The Splendid Journey*
Bill Naughton: *The Goalkeeper's Revenge; A Dog Called Nelson; My Pal Spadger*
E. Nesbit: *The Railway Children; The Story of the Treasure Seekers*
E. Neville: *It's Like this, Cat*
Mary Norton: *The Borrowers*
Wilfrid Noyce: *South Col*
Robert C. O'Brien: *Mrs Frisby and the Rats of NIMH; Z for Zachariah*
Scott O'Dell: *Island of the Blue Dolphins*
George Orwell: *Animal Farm*
Katherine Paterson: *Jacob Have I Loved*